Prai GOD *First*

KIMBERLEE HUTCHERSON

ISBN 978-1-0980-1799-6 (paperback)
ISBN 978-1-0980-1800-9 (digital)

Christian Faith Publishing, Inc.
832 Park Avenue
Meadville, PA 16335
www.christianfaithpublishing.com

Printed in the United States of America

Acknowledgment

When I was about eight years old, my best friend and I skipped up the street to a neighbor's home where a Good News Club was being hosted. That day both my friend and I prayed to receive Jesus as our Lord and Savior. We did not live in Christian homes, so a decade would go by before we felt the Lord drawing us into a relationship with Him. As soon as we were able, we started attending church and pursuing our personal relationship with the Lord. I believe God had His protection over our lives until the day we could follow Him. This is why I strongly believe in the ministry of Child Evangelism Fellowship and the work they do to help little ones come to know Jesus Christ as their Lord and Savior and teaching children to praise God at an early age.

My good friends, Frank and Connie Porter, have dedicated a large part of their lives to the ministry of CEF. They continue to have such passion for what they do in CEF. It brings my heart great joy to watch them enthusiastically share the gospel and to teach children songs they will probably sing their whole lives.

This song is a particular favorite of mine. Its words are so simple, yet it says exactly what we need to do.

> Praise Him, praise Him, praise Him in the morning
> Praise Him in the noon time,
> Praise Him, praise Him, praise Him when the
> sun goes down.

I can only imagine how many young lives Frank and Connie have influenced with their genuine love for children and ministry. How fortunate I am to be a part of their lives. They have been a huge support and encouragement through this book process. You guys are awesome!

With all my love and respect,
Thank you, Frank and Connie Porter

Introduction

I started collecting praise words over twenty-five years ago when I became a part of a group called Moms-In-Touch. A group of moms meeting once a week to pray for our schools, teachers and children. When we prayed, we used the model of prayer Jesus gave in Matthew 6. We always started our prayer time by offering up praise to God. This was the perfect way to start our prayer time, except there was one issue that continued to bother me. We only used the same few praise words every week. This bothered me because we were talking about the infinite God of the universe, and all we could manage were a few words to describe God's unlimited attributes. Even in our limited English language, we should have been able to express a multitude of words praising God. I would even learn a new word I was eager to share during our group prayer time, but as we started to praise, I could not recall the word. I knew then, I had to start keeping track of the many wonderful words and verses I found dealing specifically with God's attributes. Over the years, I collected words and put them into alphabetical order so I could easily reference them. This collection now contains over five hundred praise words. Many of these words come from Scripture, but the dictionary was used as well.

My hope is, you, too, will start on your own journey collecting praise words as you seek to know God more intimately by recognizing Him in all things and offering back the praise He deserves.

> I bless God every chance I get; my lungs expand
> with His praise. (Ps. 34:1, MSG)

I will bless the Lord at all times;
His praise shall continually be in my mouth.
My soul shall make its boast in the Lord;
The humble shall hear it and rejoice.
O magnify the Lord with me,
And let us exalt His name together. (Ps. 34:1–3)

David wrote these words a long time ago, but this psalm communicates exactly what I would want the reader of this book to do. Be ready at all times to speak praises and magnify the Lord, together exalting His name. Let's have a revival of God's people coming together and committing to praising God first, focusing on His glory and offering back to Him words of praise. I believe David understood how important and powerful praise is. It is something that should be done continually and in all circumstances.

Since I am focusing on praise, I would like to point out the difference between praise and thanksgiving. When we are being thankful, we are acknowledging a favor or gift. Also, it can be an expression of gratitude. Praise, however, expresses warm approval of or admiration. Praise means to exalt or worship. The distinction here is thanksgiving is gratitude for something the person has done, while praise is recognizing who the person is and admiring or worshiping them for it.

When we are thankful to God, we are being grateful for what He has done and given to us. When we are praising God, it is much more personal. We are focusing on who He is, not what He has done. For example, if I thank God for His creation, that is pretty broad; it covers a lot. But if I praise God for being the creator, I'm acknowledging one of His attributes and worshiping Him for it. That's personal.

Both thanking God and praising Him are extremely important, but what I have found in my own life is I'm much better at thanking God than praising Him. It is easier for me to see the gifts God gives me and all He does for me than it is to focus completely on Him, deeply pondering who He is. I'm trying to articulate an important difference between praising and thanking so we are careful to do both. Pondering who God is requires getting to know God more intimately. The deeper we know God, the more we will want to praise Him. Like any relationship, it takes time and commitment. It is well worth it.

> Ascribe to the Lord the glory due His name;
> Worship the Lord in holy array. (Ps. 29:2)

> Through Him then, let us continually offer up a sacrifice of praise to God, that is, the fruit of lips that give thanks to His name. (Heb. 13:15)

Praising God first is our first fruit sacrifice.

Praise God First

How often do you truly praise God? Be honest with yourself. Is it once a week while singing songs at church? Maybe you listen to Christian radio and sing along. Or maybe you are someone who remembers to start your prayers with praise. But for so many, like myself, it is not the first thing that comes to mind when praying. There is a tendency to go right to what I want. It can be difficult not to be distracted and truly concentrate on offering up praises to God.

Distraction has been a subtle, but powerful, negative influence in my life. It keeps me from taking time to consider who it is I am really living for. In my often hurried prayers, I go right to my petitions without first acknowledging that I know God intimately and trust Him. I should first show God respect by praising Him using very specific words that focus on His attributes.

If you are a parent or work with children, then I am sure you have experienced at some time, a certain kind of disrespect. My kids have always provided great lessons for me. The relationship between what I desire from them and what they desire from me has to be similar to what God would desire from His children. I don't know about you, but in our household respect is very important. My husband and I do not tolerate anything less than proper respect toward others. So how does this relate to God? We must be careful to show God the proper respect. If my child were to come to me and start making demands by saying, "I want" or "Do this for me," chances are, I would not be inclined to help them. However, if my child were to start by saying something like "Hi, Mom, since I know you care, I was wondering if you would please help me with this problem?"

I believe my response would be very different. In this statement, my child recognized a character quality in me and thus, showed me respect by acknowledging it. Would God not enjoy the same kind of respect? Does He not wholeheartedly deserve it? The answer, of course, is *yes*!

So here it is, consider praising God first before making requests of Him. Be sincere. Find a word that best describes how you feel or are needing to feel about God, then offer it up to Him in praise. For example, if you are feeling anxious about something, start by praising God for being calming. Even if you don't feel calm, praise God anyway. "I praise you God for being a God of calmness." Do it and keep doing it until you feel calm. Instead of saying, "Oh, God, help me," be more specific. Praise Him for being near, committed, and concerned. Remember, God loves you and desires to have the best possible relationship with you. Praising Him is essential to that relationship.

Now consider the Lord's prayer Jesus gave in Matthew 6:9–13. It begins by recognizing God as our Father, our Abba. By starting our prayer this way, we address our Father whom we love and respect. Then Jesus says, "Who art in heaven." This recognizes God's position of authority over us and His sovereignty. Next, Jesus says, "Hallowed be Thy name." Jesus acknowledges God's holiness and honors and revers Him for it. All this is said before any requests are made. Praise is given first. This is our example. However, I want to be clear, Jesus did not intend for us to use this model of prayer as a formula guaranteeing we will get what we want. There is no way, ever, to manipulate God. We should never use praise and prayer as a form of manipulation. The Lord's prayer is an example of how we should pray, not a formula to guarantee results. There is no such formula. God is sovereign over all and in every situation.

That being said, now let's look at Matthew 6:8, "Therefore do not be like them (the gentiles); for your Father knows what you need before you ask Him." The gentiles apparently used a lot of meaningless repetition in their prayers. Jesus doesn't want us to do that. I think His preference would be to not miss praising God first. That way, if we get distracted, interrupted, fall asleep, etc., we know God's got the rest of it. That is what the verse says, "Your Father knows what you need before you ask Him." Wow! I love this. All I have to do is praise Him. The rest of the prayer is basically for my benefit. I get to have communication with God. I get to express my desires, concerns, and anything else in my heart. That is great, but if for some reason I don't get to the rest of the prayer, God has already got it. I think this is freeing, at least for me, since prayer is not really my gift. I can know, if I praise God first, I've done the most important part. God has got the rest. Obviously, I am not promoting slacking on prayer. We should always have communication with God. It is super important. Just don't forget to start with praise.

> Pray, then, in this way: "Our Father who art in heaven, Hallowed be Thy name." Matt. 6:9)

Take a Stand

Why do you suppose it is so difficult to remember to praise God first? To have a multitude of wonderful words in our minds ready to offer them back to our Heavenly Father? I believe it is because we have a spiritual force working against us that desperately does not want us to praise God. Satan hates it when we praise God because when we do, we are expressing our love and adoration for Him as well as our trust in Him. There is great power in praise. Praising God releases joy in our hearts. Joy is much better than anger and bitterness. Satan wants us to be angry. When we are angry, we tend to blame God instead of praising Him. Psalm 18:30 says God's ways are blameless. Did you know that? Satan would have you believe otherwise. If you find yourself angry and wanting to blame God, praise Him for being blameless. Keep praising God for this as many times as it takes until you feel victory. Yes, you are fighting a spiritual battle! Praising God first is a weapon you need to win this battle and to replace anger, doubt and fear with joy, trust, and peace.

Remember, God has attributes that are not as popular as others, such as disciplinarian, chastiser, and refiner. He also allows things to happen on this earth we just don't understand. Some really difficult things happen that leave us questioning Him and His love for us. Know this, we serve a God Who cannot be figured out, thankfully, or He would not be a God worth praising. We need to trust and praise Him even in the most difficult of circumstances. It is hard to do when walking through the refiner's fire. It is hard to praise God for discipline, but we need to anyway. It does get easier. It shows strength of character. It shows your trust in Him and what He is doing in your life. Ultimately, you will be blessed.

> God is great, everything works together for good for his servants. I'll tell the world how great and good you are. I'll shout Hallelujah all day, everyday. (Ps. 35:27–28, MSG)

> Then the Lord said, "Because this people draw near with their words and honor Me with their lip service, but they remove their hearts far from Me, and their reverence for Me consists of tradition learned by rote," [*Rote* means "a memorizing process using routine or repetition without full comprehension"] (Isa. 29:13 NASB)

When you are praising God, be sincere. Be real. He is not interested in empty words you do not understand, or in memorized prayers you routinely repeat without thought to what you are saying. He wants your heart to be in it. He wants you to know exactly what you are praising Him for. God wants you to be honest with yourself and with Him. Please take praising God seriously. It is something you have to be deliberate about, not lukewarm. Otherwise, it probably won't happen because Satan does not want it to. Satan has schemes, and we are supposed to stand firm against the schemes of the devil, the schemes being to rob us of our joy and peace. He uses all kinds of tactics to do this: sadness, hurt, frustration, fear, anger. These are all emotions that make it difficult to feel like praising God. This is exactly when it is so important to take a stand, not letting the devil have opportunity to steal the chance to show God we trust Him even if our emotions are not in agreement. You see, it is not just about praising God when we are happy and feeling good (though this is important too). We must choose to praise Him first every day no matter how we might be feeling. "God, I praise You for being my light in the darkness. God, I praise You for being my burden carrier. God, I praise You for being my advocate." Get the idea? I'm choosing to praise God for His attributes rather than complain about my problems. By doing this, I'm showing God I love, honor, and trust Him no matter the circumstances.

I feel very passionate about praising God first because I know it works. It works when you are facing a spiritual battle; it works when you are confused and scared; it works anytime, anywhere, and in every situation. Not only that, but it develops a wonderful intimacy with our Father.

To know someone intimately, you must spend time with them and find out what makes them who they are, exploring the things about their personality that makes them unique and special. If I am willing to invest the time, I can find out interesting things about an individual that eventually leads to a more intimate relationship with them. The same is true for our relationship with God. The words that are in this book will help you see how amazing our Father is. As you read these attributes of God and offer up praise to Him for these attributes, you will develop a deeper level of intimacy with Him. Intimacy is a wonderful thing to share with our Heavenly Father. Nothing can replace it!

When we are very specific about our praise toward God, I believe it is more meaningful to Him. I know that if someone selects a specific attribute of mine and then compliments me on it, it is more meaningful to me because they have taken the time to recognize, acknowledge, and appreciate who I am. Who doesn't enjoy this? So it should be no surprise God would enjoy this too. After all, He created us in His image. We can please God merely by recognizing His attributes, acknowledging them and then offering back our appreciation for who He is. This is the reason for the list of some of God's attributes—so we have a tool to help us be more specific in our praise, therefore drawing nearer to Him. Specific praise to God shows Him the respect and glory due His Name.

I have found it very helpful to keep this list of some of God's attributes handy so I can refer to it often. It is meant to be used as a quick reference to a multitude of amazing words that just begins to describe the depths and vastness of our magnificent God.

> But as for me, the nearness of God is my good; I
> have made the Lord God my refuge, That I may
> tell of all Thy works. (Ps. 73:28)

Practice Praise

And it came about while He was on His way to Jerusalem, that He was passing between Samaria and Galilee.

And as He entered a certain village, ten leprous men who stood at a distance met Him;

and they raised their voices saying, "Jesus, Master, have mercy on us!"

And when He saw them, He said to them, "Go and show yourselves to the priests." And it came about that as they were going, they were cleansed.

Now one of them, when he saw that he had been healed, turned back, glorifying God with a loud voice,

and he fell on his face at His feet, giving thanks to Him. And he was a Samaritan.

And Jesus answered and said, "Were there not ten cleansed? But the nine—where are they?

"Was no one found who turned back to give glory to God, except this foreigner?"

And He said to him, "Rise, and go your way; your faith has made you well." (Luke 17:11–19, NASB)

One out of ten men healed of leprosy went back to praise God. As a result, Jesus said he was made well. The man had already been healed of leprosy, so Jesus must have been referring to something else, probably his soul. But regardless, because of his choice to praise God for the healing, he received more blessing.

It is crazy to think how these other nine men cleansed from their disease did not give God the glory. Why did they not go with the one to praise God? Was there something more important they had to do? What could have possibly been more important than taking time to recognize what God had done for them? They were miraculously healed but couldn't be bothered to praise God for it. And then I had to ask myself, "How often do I do this?" Miss the obvious opportunity to give God the glory. I think it is pretty easy to do. We get distracted, busy, and we forget. Because of this, how many extra blessings are we missing out on? There is something we could praise God for every day, but do we? Like anything, it takes practice.

Find a praise word for the day. Focus on that attribute of God. Begin regularly praising God for that particular attribute. For instance, today I need clarity, so I'm going to praise God today for being clear. I'm also going to praise Him for being concise. Even if I'm not feeling it, I am still going to praise Him for it. I believe this keeps God close in our thoughts and shows Him we trust Him. Keep practicing praise. It is our honor to give God the glory due His name.

Express Praise Freely

And with a leap, he stood upright and began
to walk; and he entered the temple with them,
walking and leaping and praising God.
And all the people saw him walking and
praising God. (Acts 3:8–9)

Have you felt like walking and leaping and praising God lately?
Maybe not. Maybe it's been a very difficult time for you and
this is the last thing you feel like doing. Or maybe it is not your
personality to show outward expressions of praise. It does say "walk"
too. That is something you could probably do that wouldn't make
you feel uncomfortable. God doesn't require us to praise a certain
way. Dancing and leaping may not be your style, but don't use it as
an excuse to hold back. Go somewhere where you can be alone and
free to express your praise toward God any way you feel like it. Find
it within you and determine to start praising God today. It is life
changing. Look forward to the day when you actually do feel like
walking and leaping and praising God for all the people to see. Okay,
maybe not all the people, but you never know, even the most con-
servative might be tempted to shout for joy at what God has done.

Worshiping and praising God corporately with other believers
is wonderful, but it can also be done very privately. Praise can be
done anytime, anyplace. Riding in a car, standing in line, waiting in
a waiting room, sitting on an airplane, exercising, relaxing, working
in the yard, house chores, well, you get the idea.

Whatever style of praising you choose, God will be pleased if it is sincere and from your heart.

In conclusion,

praise God first because He deserves it,
praise God first because it acknowledges His glory yet remains intimate and personal,
praise God first because it reestablishes our relationship with Him,
praise God first because it acknowledges trust in Him,
praise God first because we have reason to—Jesus has saved us from our sins,
praise God first because it brings blessings to us and puts joy in our hearts,
praise God first before you get distracted and give the devil an opportunity convincing you not to,
praise God first, because we are asked to, and we want to be obedient,
praise God first because it dispels fear and doubt, and
praise God first when we pray because it shows Him our respect.

> And a voice came from the throne, saying, "Give praise to God, all you His bond-servants, you who fear Him, the small and the great." And I heard, as it were, the voice of a great multitude and as the sound of many waters and as the sound of mighty peals of thunder, saying, "Hallelujah! For the Lord our God, the Almighty, reigns. Let us rejoice and be glad and give the glory to Him, for the marriage of the Lamb has come and His bride has made herself ready." (Rev. 19:5–7)

What if we could be the multitude coming together right now to praise His Holy name? What if we are the bond servants who fear Him, the small and the great? What if we are the ones having the voice of many waters and the sound of mighty peals of thunder, saying, "Hallelujah! For the Lord our God, the Almighty, reigns?"

Wouldn't it be awesome if God's people all over the world committed to praising God first every day? No more being complacent but aggressive in our praise. Being proactive instead of reactive. I bet we would see God's blessings in a mighty way.

So you see, if we choose to praise God first, everyone comes out a winner. Who doesn't want joy in their hearts, God's blessings, and an intimate, trusting relationship with our Heavenly Father? Nothing but good comes from praising God, so why not give it a try?

Practice praise. It does make perfection.

The Lord is compassionate
and gracious, slow to anger
and abounding in
lovingkindness.
Psalm 103:8

Abounding

A *bounding* means "to be fully supplied."

Psalm 103:8 says the Lord is abounding in loving-kindness. That means we are fully supplied with the Lord's loving-kindness. Are we really? Well, that is what the Bible says. If you believe the Bible is the truth, then you must believe we are fully supplied with God's loving-kindness.

There was a time in my life when I didn't believe anyone really loved me. I didn't feel that anybody knew me in an intimate way; therefore, they couldn't possibly have loved who I was. I wanted to be known. I wanted to be loved for exactly who I was, not for someone's idea of who they thought I should be. But looking back on that time in my life, I would have to admit, I didn't even know who I was. Not really. I mean, I've grown up a lot since then. I have learned a few things along the way. One of the main things I have learned is that God has always abounded in love toward me. Back before I knew much about myself, God knew me in an intimate way. He knew the desires of my heart. He knew my love language and how I needed to be loved. He knew my strengths and weaknesses. He knew what my spiritual gift was and how I could use it. He already knew where I would fail and where I would succeed and so much more. He knew all the stuff about me that really matters.

The good news is, even though a lot has changed about me over the years, God still knows me in an intimate way and is still fully supplying me with His loving-kindness. I just wish I had known back then how to praise God for His abounding love for me. Even if I didn't feel it, if I had chosen to praise God anyway, it would not have taken long for me to feel filled with His love, contentment, and peace. It took some time to get there, but I now know I will always have God Who knows me intimately and has abounding love for me.

I praise You, God, for Your abounding lovingkindness. I am fully supplied.

A

Abba—Romans 8:15, Galatians 4:6

Abide—John 15:4, John 15:7

Ablaze—Exodus 3:2

Able Ephesians 3:20, 2 Corinthians 9:8

Abolisher—1 Corinthians 15:24, 26

Abounding—Psalm 103:81, Corinthians 15:58

Above—Ephesians 1:21, John 3:31

Absolute—Not to be doubted

Abundant—Psalm 5:7, Psalm 36:8

Accessible—Ephesians 3:12, Ephesians 2:18

Accomplished/er—Isaiah 41:4, Luke 18:31

Accurate—Having no errors

Action/Active—Hebrews 4:12

Adonai—The Lord—Psalm 35:23

Advocate—1 John 2:1

Affectionate—Philippians 1:8, Deuteronomy 10:15

Ageless—Ephesians 3:21

All In All—Colossians 3:11

Almighty—Genesis 35:11, Revelation 1:8

Alpha—Revelation 1:8, Revelation 22:13

Always—Revelation 1:4

Am—Exodus 3:14

Amazing—Acts 10:45, Acts 12:16

Amen—Revelation 3:14

Among (us)—Hosea 11:9

Ancient of days—Daniel 7:9

Anointed—Luke 7:46

Approachable—Matthew 11:28

Artist—Genesis 2:7, 22

Assurance—Hebrews 10:22

Astonishing—Psalm 33:8

Astounding—Mark 5:42

Atonement—Romans 5:11

Audible—Genesis 3:8–10

Author—Hebrews 12:2

Avenger—Romans 13:4, 1 Thessalonians 4:6

Aware—Luke 8:46

Awesome—Nehemiah 1:5, Job 37:22

Psalm 50:2

Out of Zion,
the perfection of
beauty, God
has shone forth.

Beautiful

*B*eautiful is defined as "a quality that delights the senses and exalts the mind." Psalm 50:2 says that God shines forth the perfection of beauty.

I believe that God made us with a desire to gaze on beauty because He is the perfection of beauty. When we see beauty, we see Him. Through beauty, our senses are delighted, and our minds are lifted to a higher place. It is desirable because God is there in the higher place. There is a sense of joy that is hard to describe. For me, it is the feeling I get when sitting on the end of an old pier that extends into a calm lake. I can hear the water gently lapping up against the boards. Off in the distance, I might hear the sound of a motor boat moving to a new fishing spot. The air temperature is about seventy-two degrees, with a soft breeze making for perfect comfort. The warm sun is welcome on my skin. My feet, dangling in the water, are being caressed by the movement of the gentle waves. There are no bugs, which allows me to be perfectly relaxed. The earthy smells of fresh-cut grass and pine needles are natural aromatherapy. This is my higher place, and I know God is there.

Beauty is all around us. As a photographer, I have trained myself to see beauty in the most unlikely places as well as the obvious ones. It is amazing the beauty that can be found if you are looking for it. God gives us moments of reprieve from the dullness and routine of life when we notice beauty. He made beautiful people, places, and things for our benefit. God also gave us the ability to create beauty, so we can see God's presence in our lives. He didn't have to do this, but He did. He loves us that much.

I am so blessed to be able to live in the mountains. For me, being in the mountains, experiencing their grandness and the majesty of tall jagged peaks causes me to want to praise God. I feel my mind being lifted to a higher place. I feel joy in my heart.

Maybe the mountains don't do it for you. Maybe it is the ocean, with its powerful waves. Or a thick forest full of wildlife. Or it could be a perfectly manicured green golf course. Maybe it is the peace and quiet of your own backyard. Whatever it is, seek it out. Allow yourself to be transformed by beauty, even if it is just for a moment. Allow your senses to be delighted. Notice the feeling that comes over you. There is a good reason why you like it there. See God in it and then praise Him for it. God is the perfection of beauty.

Lord God, I praise You for creating beauty and for being the perfection of it.

B

Baptizes—Ephesians 4:4–5
Beautiful—Isaiah 4:2, Psalm 50:2
Before all things—Genesis 1:1
Beginning—Colossians 1:18, Revelation 3:14
Begotten—John 3:16
Beloved—Matthew 3:17, Ephesians 1:6
Blameless—Psalm 18:30, Psalm 51:4
Boundless—Without limit, infinite
Bountiful—Psalm 13:6
Bread of life—John 6:33
Bridge (Holy Spirit)—Romans 8:26–27
Bright—Revelation 22:16, Isaiah 60:1–3
Brilliant—Vivid in color, glorious
Broad—Psalm 119:96
Burden carrier—Psalm 81:6, Psalm 55:22

Creativity

I know God is the Creator. This is fully revealed in Genesis 1 and 2. It is not difficult to praise God for being the Creator, but have you pondered and praised Him specifically for His creativity? God is so wonderfully creative. It is astounding what He created for us to enjoy.

I have never considered myself a birder or someone who really studies birds. Basically, I haven't had time for one more hobby. But as I get older, I find myself putting food out for the birds because I'm hoping they will come and hang out for a while. That way I can take notice of all the different colors and sizes. I had no idea of the many different kinds of birds. I had to really pay attention to the details before I understood how amazing birds are. No wonder people enjoy bird watching so much. Some of their feathers are magically iridescent, like a rainbow of color. Some of their beaks are long, some short, and so on. Not only are they beautiful, they all have unique sounds. The sound a wild turkey makes during his mating ritual is like the sound of a timpani drum. It is just awesome. It's such a pleasure to watch and listen to God's delightful creation of birds.

What is the point of most birds? Why are they here? Why did God make them? It is true, some are used for food, but I think most are here for our pleasure. We can gaze at them and ponder God's spectacular creativity. There is something calming about this activity because you have to be quiet and still, which is a great time to focus on God.

What about flowers? There are thousands of different kinds. Can you imagine the creativity it took to design all the various species? The intricacy and colors of these beautiful pieces of art boggles the mind. Some of the petals are velvety and soft. Some are pokey and hard to touch. Some of them smell wonderful while others do not. You get the idea. Flowers are some of my favorite things to photograph. I get to study them up close noticing how incredible they are. I see clearly God's creativity when I look closely at them. They put a good feeling in my heart.

> Consider the lilies, how they grow; they neither
> toil nor spin; but I tell you, even Solomon in all
> his glory did not clothe himself like one of these.
> (Luke 12:27)

I believe God wants us to take a closer look at His creativity. As Luke says, "Consider." Just like you might do when studying a piece of artwork. It is very pleasurable to notice the details of God's creative handiwork. Give Him that consideration. As you do, praise Him for it. Remember, He created birds and flowers using His amazing creativity for us, designed specifically for our pleasure. Let us praise Him often for it.

God, I praise You for Your awesome creativity. This is a special gift from You.

C

Calming—Matthew 8:26

Capable—Matthew 9:28

Caring—Genesis 50:24, 1 Peter 5:7

Causes—Romans 8:28

Certain—Revelation 2:17–18

Champion—Romans 8:31, Is. 19:20

Chastiser—Revelation 3:19

Christ—Acts 2:36, Matthew 16:16

Cleanses—Matthew 8:3, 1 John 1:7

Clear/Clarity—Romans 1:20, 1 Corinthians 14:33

Clever—Originality

Close—Psalm 34:18

Comforter—Psalm 23:4, 2 Corinthians 1:3

Committed—Joshua 1:5

Companion—Joshua 1:5

Compassionate—Psalm 111:4, Deuteronomy 4:31

Complete—Colossians 2:10

Concerned—Matthew 9:36

Concise—Expressing much in few words—Exodus 3:14

Confidence—Psalm 71:5

Confounding—Joshua 10:10, Is. 19:3

Consolations—Job 15:11

Constant—Joshua 1:9

Consuming fire—Deuteronomy 4:24, Exodus 24:17

Controller—Power to regulate, direct

Counselor—Psalm 33:11, Psalm 73:24

Courage—John 16:33, Matthew 9:2, 22

Covers—Psalm 32:1, Proverbs 10:12

Covenant Keeper—Matthew 26:28, Luke 22:20

Creativity—Genesis 1

Creator—Isaiah 40:28, 1 Peter 4:19

Crowned—Hebrews 2:9

Cures—Luke 7:21, Luke 13:32

But the Lord
is with me
like a
dread champion

Jeremiah 20:11

Dread Champion

Dread—Fear greatly, To hold in awe or reverence.

Champion—One that holds first place, One who defends another person, warrior, superior to all others. (Taken from the *American Heritage Dictionary*)

But the Lord is with me like a dread champion; Therefore my persecutors will stumble and not prevail. (Jer. 20:11)

In other words, God, a most fierce warrior, is at my side. Wow! What a verse. How comforting to know I have a fierce defender at my side. Praise God for being a dread champion, for being superior to all others.

I have had times in my life when I really needed things to go a certain way but felt like all the cards were stacked against me, like it would take a miracle for it to work out. During these times, I have found it difficult to even pray. There is an angst in my being, which is extreme anxiety and a loss of clarity, causing a distrust in God for the way He has chosen to handle the situation. I feel as if somehow I could handle it better if only I had control. The truth is, I don't have control, and I never did. But God does, and He always has. It is always better His way, but that is a difficult thing to convince myself of when I am in pain.

Pain often causes us to take matters into our own hands. This reaction seldom turns out good. It shows a lack of trust in God and

His plan. There are many stories in the Bible that show people taking matters into their own hands with devastating results. I think of David in 1 Samuel 21–22. Because of his deceit, a whole village of people were killed. David did acknowledge and own up to his sin, which restored his favor with God. David went on to do many great things. He did not let his failures define him. God knew his heart. However, if David had remembered that God was his dread champion and trusted Him completely, then the village people would have been spared.

Our reaction to any situation should be to trust God and His plan. Trust in God is never misplaced. He is our fierce defender, our dread champion.

> You shall not dread them, for the Lord your God is in your midst, a great and awesome God. (Deut. 7:21)

Choose to praise God for being your dread champion. Even if you start out not really believing it. The fact is, He is! Fight the urge to blame God. Trust Him.

I praise You, God, for being my dread champion.

D

Daddy—Galatians 4:6
Dazzling—Song of Solomon 5:10
Decisive—Proverbs 16:33
Deep—Psalm 36:6, Romans 8:26
Defender—Zechariah 9:15
Deity—Colossians 2:9
Delightful—Proverbs 12:22
Deliverer—1 Thessalonians 1:10, Psalm 68:20
Dependable Psalm 121:8
Deserving—Revelation 4:11
Designer—Exodus 31:3–4
Desirable—Psalm 19:10
Destroyer—Revelation 11:18
Detailed—Psalm 139:1–4
Devoted—Psalm 121:2–3
Disciplinarian—Proverbs 3:11–12
Divine—Romans 1:20, Acts 17:29
Dominion—1 Chronicles 29:11
Dread Champion—Jeremiah 20:11
Dwells, Dwelling place—Psalm 90:1

Energy:
Strength in
action

Energy: Strength in Action

Do you not know? Have you not heard? The everlasting God, the Lord, the Creator of the ends of the earth does not become weary or tired. His understanding is inscrutable. He gives strength to the weary, And to him who lacks might He increases power. (Isa. 40:28–29)

I love the way these verses from Isaiah start. It is almost like Isaiah is saying, "Hello! Pay attention here." Isaiah really wants us to know, the everlasting God does not get weary or tired. He wants us to know, the One Who created us is willing to give us strength and power.

Do you realize you have access to an unlimited energy source? God wants us, and is willing for us, to tap into His energy. So why are people choosing not to use His energy source? For some, they might not realize they can. For others, though, they have become very comfortable in their laziness. They don't want to make a change, choosing rather to make excuses for their complacency.

Look, I'm not saying we shouldn't have days of rest. Obviously God knew we would need rest on a weekly basis. That is why He established the Sabbath day. Our bodies do need a recovery time. But we must be careful not to fall into the trap of long term laziness. This is not healthy for us and can lead to serious consequences.

Proverbs 23:20–21 warns, "Do not be with heavy drinkers of wine, or with gluttonous eaters of meat; For the heavy drinker and glutton will come to poverty, and drowsiness will clothe a man with rags."

It is clear that heavy drinking, overeating, and laziness are not what God would want for us. This is destructive to our bodies. It zaps us of our energy.

God says His energy does not run out. Remember, energy is strength in action. He is always in action for us. I believe He wants us to be active for Him. Laziness is a ploy Satan uses to keep us from doing this.

Read Isaiah 40 and see. God is more than capable of restoring energy to our bodies. Plug into it. Start by praising God regularly. Even when you don't feel energetic, praise Him anyway. See if you don't start gaining new strength, mounting up with wings like an eagle, running and not growing tired, walking, and not becoming weary.

Try praising God for His strength, power, and energy. I believe this action puts you on the offensive team. By doing this, you will be taking a stand against the schemes of the devil. Laziness and the lack of energy is one of his schemes.

Choosing to praise God for something you don't necessarily feel is an act of faith. God loves it when we show our faith and trust in Him. He rewards our efforts.

Isaiah 41:10 says, "Do not fear, for I am with you; Do not anxiously look about you, for I am your God. I will strengthen you, surely I will help you, Surely I will uphold you with My righteous right hand."

I praise You, Lord God, for Your energy.

E

El Elyon (God Most High)—Genesis 14:19
Elohim(Creator)—Psalm 35:23
El Roi (God Who sees)—Genesis 16:13
El Shaddai (Almighty)—Genesis 17:1
Emmanuel—Matthew 1:23
Emotion—Luke 22:39–44
Endless—Revelation 1:18
Energy—Isaiah 40:29
Enough—Colossians 2:10
Entire—Colossians 2:9
Essence—True substance
Essential—Philippians 4:13
Eternal—Romans 1:20
Ethereal—Heavenly, Spiritual
Everlasting—Isaiah 40:28, Genesis 21:33
Everywhere—In all places
Exact—Isaiah 45:18
Exalted—Hebrews 7:26
Excellent—Psalm 150:2
Exchanger—Trading our sorrow for joy
Exhilarating—Isaiah 55:12
Existent—Acts 17:28
Expression Isaiah—55:8–9
Extravagant Irregular—Fantastic

I

have called

you friends

Jesus

Friend

Aperson one knows, likes, and trusts; a favored companion; a comrade.

Jesus calls us His friend. It is true. He actually chose us to be His friend. This is an amazing statement and awesome to think about. You can read about it in John 15. Now ask yourself, "Have I made Jesus my friend?" We talk about Jesus like He is our friend. We sing about Him being our friend, but have we treated Him like a friend?

I have known a special friend my whole life. Oftentimes I would hear her say, "Me and Jesus are buds. We walk and talk." Now she wasn't being disrespectful toward Jesus. She was not forgetting His position as Lord, but it was obvious to me she considered Jesus her close friend, someone she trusted and enjoyed spending time with. I would see this close relationship she had with Jesus and wonder, "Do I have that kind of friendship with Him?"

Well, honestly, no, I did not.

I had no problem seeing Jesus as my Savior. It is a wonderful feeling to know you are forgiven and saved from eternal punishment for sin because of Him. I also had no problem seeing Him as my Lord, knowing He has full authority over my life. But friend? I trusted Him, but did I see Him as a favored companion, a comrade? I didn't know.

I thought about some of my friendships with other people. I considered what it was that set them apart from other relationships. Why did I want to spend time with them? Why did I like them? With these thoughts in mind, I began to look at how I was going to treat Jesus so I would consider Him my friend.

The definition of a friend starts with a person you know and like. So first, I started getting to know Jesus more intimately. I did this by reading about Him. I read the New Testament straight through like I was reading a good novel. I thought hard about Him the entire time I was reading. I saw things about Him I hadn't seen before. I found out I really do love who Jesus is and how amazing He is.

Next, I made a deliberate point to invite Jesus along when I was doing something fun. It has been great sharing my experiences with Him. I believe He likes to be a part of our lives at all times, not just when we need Him. Our earthly friends would probably not appreciate it if we only called on them when we needed them and never have them be a part of the fun stuff. We need to extend that same courtesy to Jesus.

Finally, to maintain a level of intimacy with Jesus, I made sure to thank Him, sing about Him, talk about Him, study Him, share Him, trust Him, love Him, and of course, praise Him first and often. None of these things are hard to do. In fact, it will become the desire of your heart, as it did mine.

Good and lasting friendships are not one sided. It requires effort on both sides. Jesus has done His part by already considering us His friend. Now we need to do our part. The benefits are worth it. I can guarantee it will be awesome when you make Jesus your friend. Praise Jesus for His friendship.

> Greater love has no one than this, that one lay
> down his life for his friends. (John 15:13)

I praise You, Jesus, for laying down Your life for me and calling me friend.

F

Fair—Psalm 145:9

Faithful—Deuteronomy 7:9, Revelation 19:11

Father of lights—James 1:7

Father of Jesus—2 Corinthians 1:3

Father of Mercies—2 Corinthians 1:3

Fills us Ephesians—5:18

Final—Isaiah 45:6–7

Fire/Flame—Isaiah 4:5

First—Revelation 1:7, Colossians 1:18

Forever—Psalm 29:10, Psalm 92:8

Forgiver—Mark 2:7, Psalm 99:8

Fortress—Psalm 71:3B, Psalm 18:2

For us—Romans 8:31

Foundation—2 Timothy 2:19

Fountain of life—Psalm 36:9

Freedom giver Galatians 5:1

Friend—John 15:14–15

Fulfills—Psalm 145:19, Luke 22:37

Fun—Induces enjoyment

Guide: One who shows the way by leading or directing; an example or model to be followed

In your unfailing love you will lead the people you have redeemed. In your strength you will guide them to your holy dwelling. (Exod. 15:13)

"For I know the plans that I have for you," declares the Lord, "plans for welfare and not for calamity to give you a future and a hope." (Jer. 29:11)

I worked as a ski instructor at the same ski area for twenty two years. During that time, I got to know the terrain of that ski area very well. I knew where it was steep and where it was mild. I knew the ski trails covered in moguls and the ones that stayed groomed. I also knew the ravines, trees, and best places to ski powder. When people took my class, they had the benefit of a knowledgeable guide to get them safely around the mountain. I would make sure we didn't go into terrain too steep or dangerous, yet challenge their abilities and guide them into becoming a better skier.

There was a problem, though. Most people taking lessons did not know me. They did not know I had years of experience and could be trusted. There are a lot of fears that show up in skiing no matter what level skier you are. That is why it was very important that I establish trust in me as their instructor and guide. They needed to know I was going to take care of them, keep them safe, while teaching them something to improve their skiing.

It was such an interesting process watching people struggle with trust issues. Some people had no problem trusting me. They allowed themselves to rest in my knowledge and abilities to take care of them. This always allowed for a good experience and a fun time. There was no time wasted on a lack of trust. For others, though, it took much longer for them to relax. They had a strong need to be in control; therefore, it was more difficult for them to let me lead. They would constantly question where I was taking them, why I was wanting them to do a certain activity, why we were going slowly, etc. It was their fears keeping them from putting their confidence in me. After a while, they would start to trust me and relax. But let's just say their experience would have been better, with a lot less time wasted, if they had trusted me from the beginning.

Then occasionally there were people who refused to trust me at all. They were not interested in doing any of the skills that would help them become better skiers. Even after I would communicate with them why we were doing a particular activity, they still had no interest in trying it. For various reasons, these people were virtually unteachable. They did not understand the process it took to be a better skier. Sometimes you have to take a few steps backward before you can move forward. Sometimes the old habits have to be broken before you can progress on the right path. This can be very challenging both mentally and physically. However, if a person is willing to do the work, the results will be very satisfying.

"Trust your guide," is a phrase I would often use with my clients. Then one day I realized God was speaking the same thing to me. He wanted me to trust Him the same way I wanted trust from my students.

God knows the terrain. He has been there before. He knows where to take me so I will have the best possible experiences in life. Sometimes this means I will be out of my comfort zone. It may be scary. It may hurt, but if I am trusting my Guide (God), then I know this is where I need to be. This is what I need to be doing in order to be better or to grow.

God is the ultimate guide. He knows everything. He leads His people in the way they should go. Unfortunately, we do not always want to go His way. We do not trust what He is doing in our lives and where He is leading us, so we choose a different path. Our path may work out okay, but God's path is so much better.

It is essential to trust God to guide you if you want the best possible experience out of life. Rest in Him. Relax and have some fun. God has got this.

> When my spirit was overwhelmed within me,
> Thou didst know my path. (Ps. 142:3)

I praise You, God, for being my trustworthy guide.

G

Generous—Psalm 116:7
Genius—Exceptional mental and creative power
Gentle—2 Corinthians 10:1
Gifts—Romans 6:23
Giver—Acts 17:25
Glorious—Psalm 145:5
Glory of Israel—1 Samuel 5:29
God—Psalm 90:2, Deuteronomy 7:9
Goodness—Psalm 25:8
The Goal—Philippians 3:14
Gracious/Grace—Isaiah 30:19
Great—John 15:13, Revelation 15:3
Guardian—1 Peter 2:25
Guide—Exodus 15:13, Jeremiah 29:11

Hallelujah !
Salvation and glory
and power
belong to our
God

Hallelujah—Expression of praise or joy

> After these things I heard, as it were, a loud
> voice of a great multitude in heaven, saying,
> "Hallelujah! Salvation and glory and power
> belong to our God. (Jer. 29:11)

H allowed—To set apart as holy, consecrate, and revere. To honor
as being holy.

> Pray then in this way: Our Father who art in
> heaven, hallowed be thy name. (Matt. 6:9)

I have been a member of two churches in my lifetime. Both were nondenominational Bible preaching community churches. After visiting many other types of churches, I found this type of church best suited for my personality and spiritual needs.

However, we are all created differently. What is good for me isn't necessarily good for you. That is why it is wonderful there are so many options to choose from when selecting a place to worship.

I have visited churches that have very specific prayers and rituals that are recited during the service. I believe people find comfort in knowing what to expect each week. Maybe this was how they were raised. It might not feel right to worship another way.

Then there are churches on the opposite end of the spectrum. These churches have high-energy, boisterous worship services that do not seem to follow any specific agenda. I believe people choose to worship here because they enjoy the freedom these church services offer.

However you choose to worship, it is all good as long as the focus is entirely on our triune God the Father, the Son (Jesus), and the Holy Spirit. They are the only Ones deserving of our worship and praise. Our amazing three-in-one God should always be at the center of worshiping. Worshiping is our time to align ourselves with what is already going on in heaven.

I remember when I was on a mission trip to Moscow, Russia. The group I was with took a day trip out of the city to a monastery about a two-hour drive away. We were going there to visit because our guide wanted us to see this very old (about 1,200 years) and still active church.

After we made our way into the walls of the monastery, we walked around the grounds, which contained the burial site of most of the czars. We then entered the church, and I was immediately overwhelmed by the serious and somber atmosphere present in the building. I became very aware I was experiencing something very different than the feeling I had while in Moscow. That feeling was more of a spiritual oppression, which felt heavy and depressing. Here in this magnificent structure, it was more like standing on holy ground.

I felt like an intruder. I was an American tourist with a large camera around my neck in a Russian orthodox church. I stuck out like a sore thumb. I doubt too many Americans had found their way out to this remote monastery. In fact, I never saw one other American tourist in the two weeks I was in Moscow. Regardless, nobody seemed bothered by my presence, so I continued farther into the church.

Every square inch of the interior walls of this amazing structure was covered with icons, paintings and frescos. It was stunningly beautiful. I stood gazing at the ancient art wondering who created them and when. I remember thinking how completely blessed I was to be there viewing what few people had.

Then I heard a sound like no other sound I had heard before. The acoustics in that place were fantastic. What I was hearing was almost indescribable. You could literally feel the sound inside you.

Like a deep vibration moving through your body. Like standing next to a timpani drum while it was being played.

Seated in a dark corner toward the front of the church were about twelve men draped in monk's robes. The sound was emanating from that corner. The men were the ones making the sound. I thought, *Oh wow! This is the real deal.* These are real monks doing what monks do, chanting. I could not understand what they were chanting, but apparently it didn't matter. The tears started rolling down my face as I experienced the sheer sacredness of that moment.

Until that time, I had not really considered God's holiness. I am sure I only received a tiny glimpse of His holiness that day, but it was enough for me to understand it was awesome. Really, there are no words. I feel I have a little better understanding of how Moses must have felt on Mount Sinai. In Exodus 3, God spoke to Moses from the midst of a burning bush. Moses was told to remove his sandals as a sign of respect. Moses was standing on holy ground.

Who knew that somewhere in Russia, a communist country, I would have such a powerful Holy God experience? The reverence displayed in that church was something very special. It was a feeling of profound awe and respect I think gets lost in our modern American churches.

Don't get me wrong, I love my church and the way it communicates God's love and forgiveness toward others. I just wish everyone, at least once, could experience that kind of reverence toward our Holy God. For me, it showed just Who it is I am worshiping. Yes, God is close and intimate, but He is also Holy God of the universe. We should never forget this. Try focusing on God's holiness and praise Him for it. It will stir your heart.

Hallelujah! I praise Your holy name. Hallowed be Thy name. Again, Hallelujah!

H

Hallelujah—Revelation 19:1
Hallowed—Matthew 6:9
Hands—Psalm 16:11
Happiness—Ecclesiastes 9:7
Harmony—Peace/Friendship
Head—Colossians 1:18
Healer—Psalm 147:3, Acts 9:34
Hearer—Psalm 145:19, Isaiah 30:19
Heart Healer—Malachi 4:6
Heavenly—Matthew 6:14
Helper—John 14:26
Hiding place—Psalm 27:5
High above—Philippians 2:9
High Priest—Hebrews 7:26
Holiness—Exodus 15:11, Hebrews 7:26
Holy Spirit—1 Thessalonians 4:8
Honor—Revelation 5:13
Hope—Psalm 71:5
Host (Lord of)—Psalm 80:7, Psalm 84:1
Humble in heart—Matthew 11:29

Praise God
for being
interesting

Interesting

Have you ever talked to someone you found really interesting? What set this person apart, causing you to pay attention to what they were saying? Maybe you found this person interesting because they introduced you to something new and different. Or maybe it was their life experiences that piqued your interest. It could be they had knowledge in a field of study or hobby you were interested in. Think about it for a minute. What do you find interesting, and why is this good?

I love talking to interesting people. Perhaps it's because for a brief time, I can live vicariously through their experiences. I can be captivated by their knowledge and maybe learn something new. Interesting people impress me because they tend to be motivated, active people using the gifts and talents God has given them. They don't necessarily have to be extraordinary. Just people who have decided to live a more abundant life Jesus talks about in the Bible.

Missionaries are a good example of this. No matter where their mission field is or was, they have stories—really interesting stories. It is always great to hear how God is working. It never gets old because it is rarely the same story. God works in mysterious ways. That is why He is so interesting. He keeps things new and different and exciting.

God created the world and all it contains. He could have made everything black and white. Instead, He gave us color. God could have made us all the same, but we are not. We are all unique. God gave us free will. We are not His minions. We have the ability to choose. This alone keeps life interesting, but He didn't stop there. He gave us senses to experience life more abundantly. Our taste, our touch, our smell, our vision, and our ability to hear are amazing gifts from God. Just think how devastating it would be to lose just one of these senses.

Think of the depths God went through to create this world we live in—the landscape in all its variations, the wildlife, the flowers, plants, and trees, colors, shapes, and sizes, varying temperatures, the elements, and so on.

Ponder any of these things and you cannot help but praise God for being interesting.

I praise You, God, for being so interesting. I'm extremely grateful for this.

> Praise the Lord! Praise the Lord from the heavens;
> Praise Him in the heights! Praise Him, all His angels;
> Praise Him, all His hosts! Praise Him, sun and moon;
> Praise Him, all stars of light! Praise Him, highest heavens,
> And the waters that are above the heavens!
> Let them praise the name of the Lord,
> For He commanded and they were created.
> He has also established them forever and ever;
> He has made a decree which will not pass away.
> Praise the Lord from the earth, sea monsters and all deeps;
> Fire and hail, snow and clouds; Stormy wind, fulfilling His word:
> Mountains and all hills; Fruit trees and all cedars;
> Beasts and all cattle; Creeping things and winged fowl;
> Kings of the earth and all peoples; Princes and all judges
> of the earth; Both young men and virgins; Old men and children.
> Let them praise the name of the Lord,
> For His name alone is exalted; His glory is above earth and heaven. (Ps. 148:1–13)

I

I Am who I Am—Exodus 3:14
Ideal—Isaiah 43:25
Illumines—1 Corinthians 2:12
Immanence—His nearness to us
Immanuel—Isaiah 7:14, Matthew 1:23
Immeasurable—Boundless
Immortal—1 Timothy 1:17
Immutable—Not susceptible to change
Impossible to lie—Hebrews 6:18
Incarnate—John 1:14
Incomparable—Unequaled
Indivisible—Deuteronomy 6:4
Indwells—1 Corinthians 3:16
Inescapable—Jonah
Inexhaustible—Matthew 11:28
Infinite—Revelation 1:8
Inhabiting Eternity—1 Peter 5:10
Innocent—Hebrews 7:26
Integrity—Isaiah 45:19
Intelligence—Psalm 145:4–5
Intense—2 Peter 3:10
Interesting—Genesis 1:1
Intimacy—Psalm 139:3
Intricate—Complex—Psalm 139:6
Invisible—1 Timothy 1:17, Hebrews 11:6
Involved—Psalm 139:13–16
Is—Hebrews 11:6

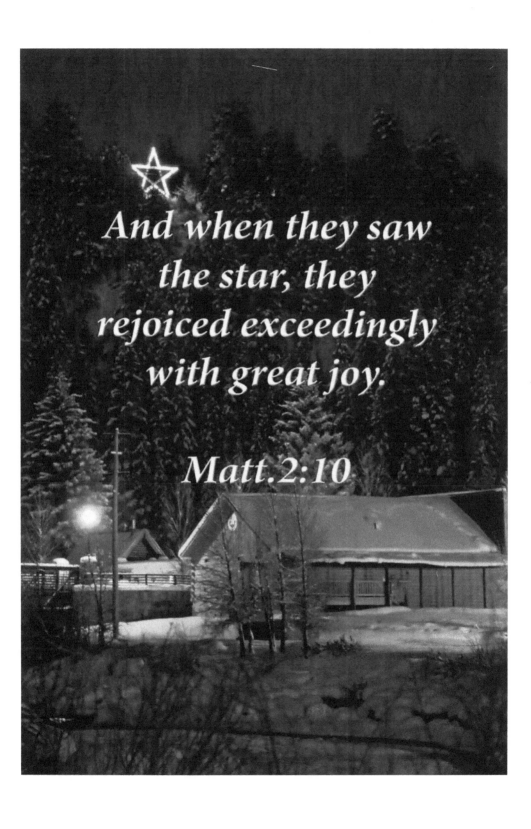

Joy: A feeling of delight, gladness, a source of pleasure

God is joy. He is the source of pleasure, gladness, and delight. John 15:11 says, "That My joy may be in you, and that your joy may be made full." True joy comes from our Heavenly Father, though the world would have us believe otherwise. Our world is filled with every imaginable way to try and bring about feelings of joy. Often we do find pleasure in our material possessions, hobbies, vacations, other people, etc., but we must consider the source of that feeling of pleasure. We might have bought the thing bringing us good feelings, but remember, God is the One Who created that feeling. He made joy for us. He didn't have to, but He wanted us to have joy in our lives. How loving of Him to do that.

How many times have we longed for a certain event to happen, and then when it did, it fell short of our expectations? Or bought ourselves something we were sure was going to bring us joy, only to find out that it didn't? Instead, it was disappointing or wasn't what we had hoped for. Then there are those times when joy comes unexpectedly. There had been no planning involved, yet there it was. Joy happened.

To me, this shows just how much God is in control of our joy. It is His joy to give and take away.

In John 15:10–12, Jesus said that if you keep His commandments (to abide in Him and love one another), that His joy will be in us and our joy may be made full. This is the source of our true joy.

So in order to have our joy be made full, we need to love Jesus, follow Him and His ways, and love people. No problem, right? Well, for some, that is true. For others, however, this can be a real struggle. For me, loving Jesus is the easy part. Loving other people can be more challenging.

I was in the customer service industry for most of my working career. When I started out, I really enjoyed people. I loved all the different personalities. I loved the way God made us all so unique. As the years went by (three decades later), I had become cynical toward others. I no longer enjoyed them. The joy I once found in people had all but disappeared. In fact, as my joy for people diminished, so did my joy in other things. I had stopped loving people; therefore, my joy was not made full. My lack of love for people was directly correlated with my lack of true joy. Jesus commands us to love one another as He loves us. To follow Jesus and His ways, I had to love people. I began to pray God would help me love people again. It took some time, but eventually my love for people returned, and so did my joy.

If it has been a while since you experienced true joy, you might want to evaluate your love for Jesus and for people. Choose to love and receive God's amazing blessing of joy.

> Then I will go to the alter of God, To God my exceeding joy; And upon the lyre I shall praise Thee, O God, my God. (Ps. 43:4)

I praise You, God, for creating joy. For being our source of true joy and for Your willingness to fill us with it.

J

Jealous—Deuteronomy 6:15, Exodus 20:5
Jehovah—Self-Existent One—Exodus 6:3
Jesus—Matthew 1:21
Jireh—The Lord Provides—Genesis 22:14
Jolly—Merry, festive—John 2:1–10
Joy/Joy giver—Psalm 51:8, 12
Judge—Psalm 50:6, Genesis 18:25
Judgment—Psalm 36:6, Ecclesiastes 12:14
Just—Romans 3:26, Proverbs 16:11

God is
acutely sensitive,
vivid, intense,
piercing, splendid,
wise, bold,
God is Keen

Keen

I love to wear a certain brand of shoes. They are well made and very comfortable. The name brand is clearly marked on every pair. Since I wear them often, I decided to look up the word to see what it meant. As I read the definition, I realized this word describes great attributes of God. The word *keen* is defined as "sharp, intellectually acute, vivid, acutely sensitive, intense, piercing, great, splendid, wise, and bold." Isn't that a great word? I love it. It has become one of my favorite praise words. I love that God is acutely sensitive and vivid.

Several years ago, I went to a friend's house to watch a movie on her brand-new high-definition television. Wow! The clarity and vividness of that television made the movie so much more enjoyable. It was captivating to watch because of the splendid, piercing colors, the clear, sharp lines, and intensity of the overall picture. I could hardly take my eyes away from it.

Now relate this to God. God is keen. He is sharp. He is acutely sensitive. Wise. Intense. He really is captivating. It is way better to keep our eyes on Him than any high-definition television. When I think of the vividness of God, His clarity, it fills me with joy and appreciation for who He is and what He has done for me. It makes me want to praise Him.

That, my friends, is the point. When we offer up praise to God, we are not just pleasing Him, we are benefiting too. Praise brings us joy by knowing we are pleasing our wonderful heavenly Father. Praising God brings focus into our lives, like using a very expensive high-end lens on our camera. The clarity and greatness cannot be matched.

I praise You, God, for being keen to our lives.

For the word of God is living and active and sharper than any two-edged sword. (Heb. 4:12)

K

Keen—Hebrews 4:12
Keeper—Psalm 121:5, Deuteronomy 7:9
Keeps—Psalm 145:20, Psalm 66:9
Kind—Psalm 145:17
King of kings—Revelation 19:16
Knowledge—Psalm 139:6, 1 Samuel 2:3
Knows—John 10:14, Jeremiah 1:4

I Am
the Light
of the
world

Jesus

Light: A source of illumination

It is the middle of January. I look outside noticing that at 5:30 p.m., I can still see daylight. This doesn't seem like much, but just one month ago it was totally dark by 5:00.

I don't like the darkness. About the only time I like it dark is when I am sleeping, watching a movie, or looking at the stars. That is why I am thankful that from now until June 21 (the summer solstice), the days will keep getting longer.

I prefer longer days and shorter nights. I get energized and motivated to accomplish various tasks due to the extra daylight. I try to squeeze every bit of useful light out of a beautiful spring or early summer day. I like to watch the sun come up, then watch it make its descent over the hills. The shadows the changing light cast over the land and the warm glow the sunset gives off makes it one of my favorite times of the day to take pictures. As a photographer, I have been chasing and studying light for as long as I can remember. At times, it seems a bit obsessive, just ask my family. I am always looking for the perfect lighting so I can have the best results with my photographs. I can tell you, though, this doesn't occur very often. Being at the right place at the right time, with the perfect light, is rare. It is very special when it does happen, and hopefully I have my camera with me to capture the moment.

Extraordinarily, there is a light that is always perfect. You don't have to chase it. This perfect light is always available to us. It is always the right time for this light. This perfect light is Jesus Christ.

John 8:12 says, "Again therefore Jesus spoke to them, saying, 'I am the light of the world; he who follows Me shall not walk in darkness, but shall have the light of life.'"

Jesus brings to our lives the perfect light we all need. He is the source of illumination into our souls, whereby we can be forgiven of our sins and cleansed of our unrighteousness. He shines into the darkness of our lives and reconciles us to God. You can read about this in John 1:4–9. And then in John 12:35–36. Salvation through Jesus Christ is available to all people. The true Light enlightens all men. We need to believe in the Light so we can become a child of the Light and then walk in the light so darkness does not overtake us.

In 2 Corinthians 4:4–6, it says that Satan blinds the minds of the unbelieving that they might not see the light of Christ, but to believers, the light shines in our darkness and into our hearts to give us the knowledge of God's glory in the face of Christ. In 1 Peter 2:9, it says that Jesus has called us out of the darkness and into His marvelous light.

> For you were formerly darkness, but now you are light in the Lord; walk as children of light. (Eph. 5:8)

> But if we walk in the light, as He Himself is in the light, we have fellowship with one another, and the blood of Jesus His Son cleanses us from all sin. (1 John 1:7)

The Scriptures are full of contrast between light and darkness. It is something we can all relate to. It is clear—we are to see the Light, believe in the Light, then walk in the Light. We don't belong in the darkness.

I am thankful I live in a place where the sun shines most of the time. This past winter, however, we had one gray day after another. I found myself getting mildly depressed. I would take walks, ski, and do things I normally did when the sun shines, but I couldn't seem to shake free of the blues. It was interesting how much the lack of sunshine affected me. I was not meant to live in darkness, or grayness for that matter, at least not for very long. It is not healthy for any of us. We all need light literally and spiritually. We need the sun, and we need the Son. Jesus is the spiritual light we need. He is the Light of the world. Without light, we die, both physically and spiritually. Without Jesus, we do not have the spiritual light we need for eternal life.

I praise You, Jesus, for being our Light. For illuminating our darkness. For allowing us to walk as children of Light. For having fellowship with us.

The next time you are enjoying the sun on your face or the sunshine through a window or seeing it shine on something, giving it that perfect glow, celebrate Jesus. Celebrate the fact that He is the Light of the world, the Light in our darkness, and the Light of our salvation.

> For Thou dost light my lamp; The Lord my God Illumines my darkness. (Ps. 18:28)

> Thy word is a lamp unto my feet, and a light unto my path. (Ps. 119:105)

L

Lamb—Revelation 5:6, 12
Last—Revelation 1:17, Isaiah 44:6
Laughter—Psalm 37:13
Leader—Isaiah 40:11
Life—Acts 17:28
Light—Psalm 27:1, 1John 1:5
Lion—Revelation 5:5
Lively—Vigorous, intense—Hebrews 4:12
Living Water—John 7:38
Logic/Logo—Speech, word, reason
Lord of Lords—Revelation 19:16
Love/Lover/Lovely—John 3:16
Loving-kindness—Deuteronomy 7:9, Psalm 36:5

Let a man regard us
in this manner,
as servants of Christ,
and stewards of
the mysteries of God.

1Cor. 4:1

Mystery

I have always enjoyed mysteries. When I was a little girl, my favorite cartoons involved solving various mysteries. I was good at guessing who the culprit was before it was revealed. I also enjoyed a board game where the object of the game was to collect clues so you could be first to solve the murder mystery. Finally, when I read, I chose books that contained a mystery of some type. As I got older, I found not much has changed. I still enjoy a good mystery. I am not sure why. Maybe it's because it arouses my curiosity for the unexplained. I enjoy the fact that life contains many mysteries. We humans do not have it all figured out, even though some might think they do. Because we don't know it all, this should keep us humble. It also keeps life interesting. We do not have to have life figured out. We can trust in the One Who does. God is the One Who created mysteries. He holds all the answers.

The Bible is full of stories of mystery. In the Old Testament, we have Noah and the ark. How in the world did he accomplish building that huge boat? How did Jonah survive in a fish's belly? How did Shadrach, Meshach, and Abednego survive the fiery furnace? I do not know, but I believe the Bible is the Word of God; therefore, I must believe these stories are true. To do this requires faith. I believe God left some things unexplained because He didn't want us to have all the answers. If we had all the answers, there would be no need for faith.

The Old Testament of the Bible spoke of a Messiah that would someday come and save the world from the punishment of sin. The mystery of who the Messiah would be and when He would arrive did not get revealed for hundreds of years later. When Jesus Christ was born, He was presented as the One Who would save people from their sins. Matthew 1:21 says, "And she will bear a Son; and you shall call His name Jesus, for it is He who will save His people from their sins." The mystery of the Messiah was solved in the person of Jesus Christ.

In the New Testament of the Bible, there are many mysteries too. While some have been revealed to us, still others remain unknown. One of them, in Ephesians 3:3–6, speaks of the fact Jews and Gentiles are equal heirs in the one body of Christ. Then in chapter 6 of Ephesians, Paul asks for prayer so he could be bold in making known the mysteries of the Gospel. The book of Revelation is indeed mysterious. You can look up the word *mystery* in your concordance if you would like to study more about mysteries in the Bible.

The point I want to make, though, is God clearly wanted us to have mystery. He chose to reveal some mysteries while keeping others hidden. It can be enjoyable to not know everything, then look back and see how God worked it all out. This is a faith builder. You can try to solve some of God's mysteries, but the truth is we may never know the answers this side of heaven. That's okay because I believe God will make known to us exactly what we need to know at exactly the right time.

In the meantime, praise God for mystery. Praise Him for the opportunity to practice faith. Practice trusting Him to reveal exactly what He wants you to know. If you find yourself feeling anxious or scared about an unknown (e.g., the book of Revelation), praise God for His mysteries. Your anxious feeling will be replaced with peace. Remember, God has always been and will always be in control. He chose to keep some things mysterious. He did this for our own good. So relax. Enjoy life a little more by trusting in God's complete knowledge of everything currently going on and everything to come.

This mystery has been kept in the dark for a long time, but now it's out in the open. God wanted everyone, not just Jews, to know this rich and glorious secret inside and out, regardless of their background, regardless of their religious standing. The mystery in a nutshell is just this: Christ is in you. Therefore, you can look forward to sharing in God's glory. It's that simple. (Col. 1:26, MSG)

The secret things belong to the Lord our God, but the things revealed belong to us and to our sons forever, that we may observe all the words of this law. (Deut. 29:29)

I praise You, God, for Your mysteries, but most of all, for revealing the mystery of the Messiah. Jesus is the One.

M

Magnificent—Noble, Exalted, Splendor, lavish

Majesty/Magnified—Hebrews 1:3, Psalm 35:27

Maker—Exodus 4:11, Psalm 95:6, Isaiah 51:13

Manifold—1 Peter 4:10, Ephesians 3:10

Marvelous—Psalm 118:23

Master—Ephesians 6:9, Matthew 8:19

Matchless—Acts 4:12

Mediator—Psalm 68:28, Hebrews 12:24

Mekoddishkem—The Lord sanctifies you

Merciful—Psalm 145:8, Lamentations 3:22

Messiah—John 1:41

Mighty One—Psalm 50:1, Luke 1:49

Mine—Psalm 31:14

Minister—Ephesians 3:19–20

Miracles/Miraculous—Exodus 34:10

Most High—Acts 16:17, Psalm 46:4, Psalm 9:2

Mystery—Colossians 1:26, Ephesians 3:4

Because of the Lord's great love we are not consumed, for His compassions never fail. They are new every morning; great is your faithfulness.

Lam.3:22-23

New

Therefore if any man is in Christ, he is a new creature; the old things passed away; behold, new things have come. (2 Cor. 5:17)

And that you be renewed in the spirit of your mind, and put on the new self, which in the likeness of God has been created in righteousness and holiness of the truth. (Eph. 4:23–24)

Therefore we have been buried with Him through baptism into death, in order that as Christ was raised from the dead through the glory of the Father, so we to might walk in newness of life. (Rom. 6:4)

Put on the new self who is being renewed to a true knowledge according to the image of the One who created him. (Col. 3:10)

God is not new; however, we should praise Him for newness of life. After reading these verses, it is clear, if we know Jesus as our Savior, we get to have a new nature or a new disposition that causes us to want to serve God and desire to do what is right. Colossians 3:10 says, "Put on the new self who is being renewed." This tells me we have to be deliberate about being renewed. It is an ongoing practice. We must continue to put on the new self so it ultimately has full authority over us. So we literally have a new nature. Our old habits and desires no longer have dominion over our choices.

If you struggle with the old self, don't give up hope. Sometimes it takes longer than we think to renew our minds. It can take time to fully understand you are a new creature in Christ. Practice renewing your mind by replacing lies with the truth about who God says you are. Start by telling yourself you are a child of the Most High God, deeply loved and forgiven.

Newness often is a process. Spring is a good example of this. Spring doesn't just show up overnight. First, the days gradually get longer. They start getting warmer too. The snow melts, leaving the ground exposed to the light and warmth. This causes the plants and flowers to start growing.

Then one day the leaves begin to emerge on the trees. It is so good to see the colors again. Newness is all around us. It went from the dull grays of winter to the vivid colors of spring. It was a process that took some time.

I believe God gave us this visual of spring to help us see what happens to us when we get saved through faith in Christ. Though our salvation happens the instant we receive Christ as our Savior, the process of changing our lives to be more like the person God intends for us to be can take time. Just like with spring, we change into something new and fresh. We go from dull grays to vivid colors. We get to put on a new self, which is in the likeness of God. We get to be new creatures. The old stuff no longer has authority over us. We get to walk in the newness of life. We get to have a new nature that desires to change and serve God.

> The Lord's lovingkindnesses indeed never cease,
> For His compassions never fail.
> They are new every morning; Great is Thy faithfulness. (Lam. 3:22–23)

These verses tell us we receive new loving-kindness and compassion from the Lord every morning. This should give us hope. He does not give up on us. No matter how bad it was before, spring always comes. Sometimes it might seem like it will never arrive, but it always does. Rest in the fact that you are a new creation, even if it doesn't feel like it yet. This is how God sees you.

Praise God for newness and the hope it brings. Jesus has made it possible for you to leave behind the winter of life and move into the spring of your life. You are never too young or too old for this process to begin.

N

Near—Psalm 34:18, Psalm 145:18
Necessary—Luke 24:26
Never Ending—Luke 1:33
Never Fails—1 Corinthians 13:8
Never leaves or forsakes—Hebrews 13:5
New, Newness—Ephesians 4:24, 2 Corinthians 5:17
Nice—Ephesians 4:32
Nissi—The Lord, my Banner
No separation—Romans 8:38–39
Now—Never too early, never late

The steps of a
man are
established
by the Lord

Order

The steps of a man are established by the Lord;
And He delights in his way. (Ps. 37:23)

Have you heard the saying, "Hindsight is twenty/twenty"? Have you ever looked back over events in your life clearly seeing God's guidance and order in it? I know I have. It is wonderful to see how God works out the steps of our lives. There is definitely order to it, even if it doesn't seem like it at the time.

The problem is, sometimes when we are in the middle of living our lives, we can become quite disordered. Life can get pretty crazy, hectic, and even out of control. If a man's steps are established by the Lord, how does this happen? Well, I think it has a lot to do with our free will God gave us to make choices. We all have free will. We all make choices. Sometimes the consequences of those choices brings about disorder. Sometimes it is the choices other people make that affect our desired order in life.

Still, somehow, God takes the mess life can be and turns it into something beautiful. He can and will bring order back into our lives. This is where faith and trust come in. Start by praising God for order in your life, in our society, and in our world.

I enjoy putting jigsaw puzzles together. I usually have one out on my table throughout winter. I like to walk by, put a couple pieces together, then move on to something else. That way, I don't feel like I'm wasting a lot of time. Some might think puzzles are a total waste of time. After all, minutes after I've put the whole thing together, I break it apart. Then it goes back in the box. So what is the point? For me, I think it is good exercise for my brain. I also find it therapeutic. It is a great visual, too, on how God can take something that seems very messy and bring order to it.

When I work a puzzle, I start by finding the border pieces, putting them together to form the frame. Then I spread all other pieces out facing up. I'm amazed at how a thousand pieces look lying on the table. It doesn't seem possible all those pieces are going to fit inside the borders. I have worked enough puzzles to know they always end up fitting. As impossible as it seems in the beginning of the puzzle, the pieces always fit, making a beautiful picture. Because of my experiences with puzzles, I have learned to trust that eventually they will all fit. Yet sometimes I question if there are pieces missing or if there was a mistake made. I'm not sure why I do this. Maybe I'm looking for reasons why I can't seem to navigate my way through the puzzle. I then have to remind myself to trust the manufacturer and the fact that the puzzle was made to fit together. The manufacturer has seen the completed picture. I have to trust it will work.

God is our manufacturer, so to speak. He has seen the completed picture. He already knows how all the pieces of our lives are going to fit together. We need to trust He will do what He says He will do. He will bring order and wholeness to our lives.

When I think of God's attribute of order, I think of the book of Ecclesiastes. Chapter 3 shows definite order to life. Verse 1 says there is an appointed time for everything. And there is a time for every event under heaven. Then verses 2 through 8 speak of all the events of life having divinely appointed times. If you haven't read Ecclesiastes 3 in a while, go ahead and give it a look. I think it shows God has put structures in our world and established the conditions in which these structures are maintained and preserved by the rule of law. This is one of the definitions of order. The word *order* has other meanings, but I am specifically referring to God's attribute of order. He is the One Who established what is right and what is wrong. He is the One Who gave us law and order.

Can you imagine what our world would be like if God had not given us order? It would be complete chaos. There would be no rules, no boundaries, nothing to measure what is right and wrong.

Thankfully, God did not leave us in complete chaos. He knew we would need order. He created us in His image. He is a God of order.

Think of your life as a puzzle with many pieces. It might be difficult to see right now how all the pieces are going to fit, but rest assured, knowing God has seen the final picture. The final picture is going to be beautiful because He knows how to make all the pieces fit.

Praise God for His attribute of order. He established order because He loves us.

> In the morning, O Lord, Thou wilt hear my voice; In the morning I will order my prayer to Thee and eagerly watch. (Ps. 5:3)

O

Observant—1 Peter 3:12, Job 34:21
Omega—Revelation 1:11
Omnipotent—Unlimited power and authority
Omnipresent—Being everywhere
Omniscient—Knowing everything
One—Ephesians 4:5–6, Deuteronomy 6:4, John 10:30
On high—Hebrews 1:3
Only God—Hebrews 11:17, 1 Timothy 1:17, Romans 16:27
Order—Psalm 37:23, Isaiah 9:7
Over All—Ephesians 4:6
Overcomes—John 16:33
Overseer (of our souls)—1 Peter 2:25
Owner of all—Psalm 50:10–12

for God is not
a God of
confusion
but of peace,
as in all the
churches
of the
saints.

1 Cor. 14:33

Peace

For God is not a God of confusion but of peace,
as in all the churches of the saints. (1 Cor. 14:33)

God is not a God of confusion or disorder. He does not enjoy disorder or confusing people. It is not His nature. God is a God of peace. He wants His children to be at peace, not confused and disordered.

Satan loves it when we are confused. His nature is disorder. He even sounds confusing. If you hear a voice in your head that sounds loud, angry, unclear, accusing, etc., this could possibly be Satan trying to confuse and disrupt harmony in your thoughts. It will not sound peaceful.

However, when God chooses to speak to us, He does it in a clear voice, not loud but noticeable. If you are unsure whether you are hearing God's voice or something else, ask yourself, "Is the sound calm, clear, and concise?" This is how God speaks to us. He is not noisy or confusing. If God wants you to hear from Him, then you will hear Him. It is up to you to believe it is Him. You might not like what He is telling you, but if you choose to listen, you will have peace knowing it is His will.

The Scriptures contain many verses telling of the peace of God, also of Jesus as the Prince of peace. God created us in His image (Gen. 1:26); therefore, we were created to be beings of peace. This is why we need peace in our lives. It is our nature.

Unfortunately, we have an enemy working to rob us of our peace, particularly when it comes to relationships with other people. Satan loves dissension among God's people. He has many ways to accomplish this dissension. Finding fault in others is one of the main traps people fall into, causing big problems in relationships. Choosing to focus on people's faults, and not their strengths, is not what Jesus wants. As Christ followers, we are to be kind, patient, loving, forgiving, and have self-control. (Gal. 5:22) We are not to keep account of wrongs suffered. If we do, we will struggle with bitterness and anger. Remember, we have all sinned and fallen short of the glory of God (Rom. 3:23). So keep this in mind when choosing to focus on people's faults and wrongs suffered. The Bible is very clear on this issue:

> So then let us pursue the things which make for peace and the building up of one another. Make choices not to hold onto bitterness, wrath, and anger. Instead, be forgiving. This is what will bring peace. (Rom. 14:19)

> For if you forgive men for their transgressions, your heavenly Father will also forgive you. But if you do not forgive men, then your Father will not forgive your transgressions. (Matthew 6:14–15)

Hebrews 12:14–15 tells us to pursue peace with all men. In 1 Thessalonians 5:13, it says to live in peace with one another. Proverbs 17:14 says starting a quarrel is like breaching a dam, so drop the matter before a dispute breaks out.

We do have a choice. We can choose to quarrel, hold on to grudges, find fault, keep track of wrongs, and be unforgiving, or we can do as the Lord would want us to do: pursue peace.

> And be kind to one another, tender-hearted, forgiving each other, just as God in Christ also has forgiven you. (Eph. 4:32)

I am convinced, if I choose to hold on to my anger and bitterness, justified or not, I will lose my peace. This is not a comfortable feeling. This is living contrary to the way God designed me to live, which is to be at peace with God and people.

If you have an unresolved dispute with another person, and it is within your power to settle the matter, then you need to pursue peace by, first, forgiving that person. I know this can be difficult. It may take time, but it is absolutely necessary to restore peace.

Next, you need to resolve to put away the grievance. This is what Ephesians 4:31 says to do. If you choose to do this, eventually your peace will be restored. Possibly your health as well.

When we are unforgiving, allowing a seed of bitterness to grow, it not only causes us to lose peace of mind, but can cause physical illness and problems with our body. This is not God's desire for us. He is a God of peace. He created us to live in peace. It is our choice.

Finally, praise God for peace. If you don't have it, then ask Him to show you why. You might not like the answer, but trust Him. Respond to Him by being willing to do what He asks. Remember, God is not a God of confusion but of peace.

I praise You, God, for Your perfect peace that surpasses all understanding.

> When we worship the right way, God doesn't stir us up into confusion; he brings us into harmony. This goes for all the churches-no exceptions. (1 Cor. 14:33, MSG)

P

Paradise—Revelation 2:7

Passionate—Ardent, adoring, intense love

Patient—2 Peter 3:9

Peace—1 Corinthians 14:33, John 14:27

Perfect—Psalm 19:7, 1 Corinthians 13:10

Perfecter—Hebrews 12:2

Permanent—Fixed and lasting

Personal—Acts 2:21, Matthew 10:40

Pleased—Matthew 11:26, John 8:29

Planner—2 Samuel 14:14

Pomp—Magnificent display/splendor

Portion—Psalm 16:5, Lamentations 3:24

Potter—Romans 9:21

Power—Luke 24:49, 1 Chronicles 29:11

Precious—Psalm 36:7

Presence—Exodus 33:14, Psalm 44:3

Present—Psalm 46:1

Preserver—Psalm 36:6, Psalm 140:1, 4

Prince of Peace—Isaiah 9:6, Acts 5:31

Promises—2 Peter 1:4, 2 Timothy 1:1

Promise Keeper—Hebrews 10:23

Propitiation—1 John 2:2

Protector—Psalm 121:7

Provider—Psalm 145:16

Pure/Purity—Psalm 12:6, Psalm 19:8

He quenches our thirst

Quench

He sends forth springs in the valleys; They flow
between the mountains; They give drink to every
beast of the field; The wild donkeys quench their
thirst. Beside them the birds of the heavens dwell;
They lift up their voices among the branches. He
waters the mountains from His upper chambers;
The earth is satisfied with the fruit of His works.
(Ps. 104:10–13)

I live in a very dry, southwest climate. There are some real advantages to living without high humidity, disadvantages too, one of them being, I wouldn't go anywhere without a water bottle. It doesn't take long before I start feeling thirsty. I need to drink water to satisfy the dryness in my mouth. I know if I don't drink, I end up dehydrated. This is not good. There are side effects such as headaches and fatigue that are not fun.

The human body is made up of around 60 percent water. The brain is composed of about 70 percent. The lungs are over 80 percent water. Clearly we need a lot of water to sustain us. Our bodies need to have water replenished regularly, especially if we are physically active. There is nothing like a cold, sweet drink of water when we are thirsty. It satisfies.

Psalm 104 says God satisfies the whole earth by bringing forth springs in the valleys and waters from the mountains. He quenches the thirst of the earth and all its living creatures.

I love how God uses the correlation between our physical need and our spiritual need to have our thirst satisfied. Jesus spoke to a woman at a well in John 4:13–14, explaining that everyone who drank from the well would thirst again. Then Jesus said that whoever drinks from the water He would give would never thirst again. He was not talking about physically. He was talking about our need for salvation. He gave Himself when He died on the cross. If we believe in Him, we will be filled with the living water, which is eternal life. We will never thirst again. This is about our souls being satisfied. We will no longer thirst for forgiveness and salvation. That thirst is quenched once and for all through the living water of Jesus Christ.

Hallelujah! Praise God for quenching our thirst with His living water. He gives to us freely. We don't have to earn it. Jesus did not require prerequisites from the woman at the well when He spoke about receiving His living water. He doesn't require any from you, either. Just believe Him and trust Him. That is all.

As long as we are alive on this earth, we will need to drink water to satisfy our physical need. But we must also satisfy our spiritual need by drinking (receiving) the living water, Jesus.

Do not neglect your spiritual thirst for forgiveness, acceptance and unconditional love. Receive Jesus today.

> As the deer pants for the water brooks,
> So my soul pants for Thee, O God.
> My soul thirsts for God,
> for the living God. (Ps. 42:1–2)

> Now on the last day, the great day of the feast, Jesus stood and cried out, saying, "If any man is thirsty, let him come to Me and drink. He who believes in Me, as the Scripture said, 'From his innermost being shall flow rivers of living water.'" (John 7:37–38)

> And He said to me, "It is done. I am the Alpha and Omega, the beginning and the end. I will

give to the one who thirsts from the spring of the water of life without cost." (Rev. 21:6)

I praise You, Lord Jesus, for being our thirst quencher.

Q

Quencher—Psalm 104:10–13
Quick—Revelation 3:11, 22:20, Romans 9:28
Quiet—1 Timothy 2:2, Zephaniah 3:17

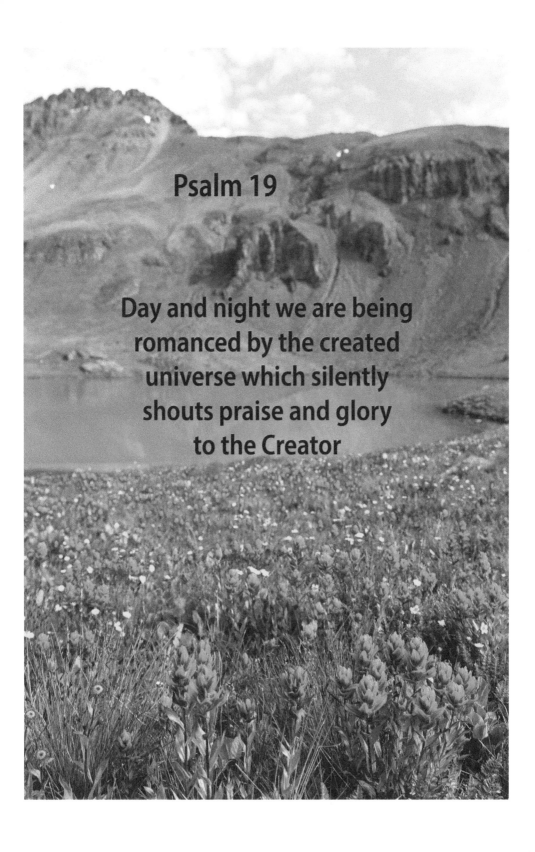

Psalm 19

Day and night we are being
romanced by the created
universe which silently
shouts praise and glory
to the Creator

Romance

I am fortunate to have quick access into the mountains surrounding my town. Whenever I'm in the mountains, no matter what season, I am filled with a unique joy. You might say I literally feel romanced by God when spending time with Him in that setting. It is like a sacred love affair that is difficult to explain. It's as if the brilliant display of colorful wildflowers were planted just for me. I find quartz crystals and other minerals that seem precisely cut into fine gemstones just for me. The azure blue of a high mountain lake with its impossibly clear, pure and cold water brings a refreshing healing to my soul. The smell of pine trees is my aromatherapy. I breath deeply filling my lungs with God's fresh clean air. Then, I expel letting out worry and stress. I love getting glimpses of all varieties of wildlife. Sometimes I am blessed to watch them at play. I am romanced by the sheer wonder of it all.

God did this for me. For all of us. Allow yourself to be romanced by Him. He knows His children. He knows their needs. Romancing us through His beauty and creation is one of the ways He meets those needs. Feeling personally loved and special is not just for young lovers. It is for anyone, at any age who is willing to ask and receive from God. Don't expect romance to come from other human beings. Though it can occur, it is not reliable. Expectations often cause disappointments. However, God, in unexpected ways, shows us His love. Be alert and sensitive to what He is doing. He can be subtle as well as grand. Personally, it is the small gestures of love shown to me on a regular basis that brings on the romantic feeling. I have to be attentive though so I don't miss His gestures of love.

I believe very strongly in giving credit were credit is due. At times I have heard people give account of how they believed a dead relative gave them a sign. It made them feel good knowing that person was looking down from above. The sign given was probably real. The feeling they received was real. But they missed God's personal love for them by not recognizing God as the One giving the sign. Give God the credit so you don't miss out on more of His signs and wonders. It's Him showing deep and personal love for you. He is the lover of your soul.

Go for a walk in a park. Go to a botanical gardens. Literally stop and smell the roses. Look at the stars. Sunsets. Laugh. Sing. Drink in the joys of life. Praise God for His romance because His romance is authentic and special. He is the designer of all that is romantic.

> The fig tree has ripened its figs, And the vines in
> blossom have given forth their fragrance. Arise,
> my darling, my beautiful one, and come along!
> (Song of Sol. 2:13)

God invites us to share in the delights of His company. I praise You, God, for adding dimension to life through romance.

R

Raah—The Lord, my Shepherd

Rabbi—Matthew 26:25, Mark 9:5

Radiance—Habakkuk 3:4, Hebrews 1:3

Radical—Acts 3:6–9

Ransomed me—Psalm 31:5, Matthew 20:28

Rapha—The Lord that heals

Reachable—Acts 2:38–39

Ready—Psalm 86:5

Real—John 1:14

Reassuring—Acts 2:21

Receivable—John 20:22, Matthew 18:5

Receptive—Matthew 18:5

Recognizable—John 20:28–29

Reconciling—Romans 5:11, Colossians 1:20

Rectify—To set right

Redeemer—Isaiah 48:17, Psalm 34:22

Redemption—Psalm 130:7, Ephesians 1:7–8

Reformer—Change for the better

Refreshing—Acts 3:19

Refuge—Psalm 59:16, Psalm 18:2,

Refiner—Psalm 12:6

Regenerates—Titus 3:5

Reigns—Psalm 96:10, Exodus 15:18

Rejuvenates—Matthew 11:29

Relational—John 1:14

Relaxer—Psalm 23:2

Release—Psalm 146:7

Relevant—John 3:16

Reliable—Hebrews 10:10, 23

Relieves/Relief—Psalm 4:1

Remarkable—Luke 5:26

Renews—2 Corinthians 4:16, Colossians 3:10

Renovates—Titus 3:3–5

Repairs—Psalm 34:18

Repays—Hebrews 10:30

Replaces—Matthew 16:24–25

Replenish—Acts 3:16

Reprove—Revelation 3:19, Proverbs 3:12

Rescuer—Psalm 81:7, Psalm 71:3

Resourceful—Philippians 4:19, Luke 24:49

Respectable—Philippians 2:9–10

Resplendent—Psalm 76:4

Responsible—Philippians 2:5–8

Responsive—Philippians 4:6–9, Psalm 20:1, 9

Rest—Matthew 11:28

Restorer—Psalm 23:3, Psalm 80:19

Resurrection—Acts 1:9–11, Philippians 3:10

Reunites—Philippians 3:20–21

Revealing—Psalm 18:28, Ephesians 6:12

Revives—Psalm 71:20, Psalm 80:18

Rewards—Hebrews 11:6, Revelation 11:18

Right—Psalm 19:8

Righteous—1 John 2:1, Psalm 145:17

Risen—Luke 24:34

Rock—1 Corinthians 10:4, Isaiah 26:4

Rock of Habitation—Psalm 71:3

Romance—Psalm 21:1–7, Psalm 19

Ruler—Acts 17:24

1 Samuel 16:7b

"For God sees not as man sees, for man looks at the outward appearance, but the Lord looks at the heart."

Sees

For God sees not as man sees, for man looks at the outward appearance, but the Lord looks at the heart. (1 Sam. 16:7)

For the eyes of the Lord move to and fro throughout the earth that He may strongly support those whose heart is completely His. (2 Chron. 16:9)

God sees our true heart. He sees everything about us. Isn't that great? Well, it's possible we're not always comfortable with this fact. Sometimes it might feel embarrassing, humiliating, or shameful. Do we want God to see everything? I think it might be human nature to try and hide certain feelings from God. Look at Adam and Eve. They desperately tried to hide their shame from God by using fig leaves to cover themselves. I have thought more than once, "How foolish of them to think they could hide from God." He knew exactly where they were and what had happened. But I have to admit, at times I too have been foolish. I have tried to hide from God. I did not use fig leaves, though. I used denial and dishonesty with myself to cover up the truth. If I refused to admit to myself I had a problem, then I was off the hook for doing something to change it. Right? Wrong! God still sees. He is not fooled. And do you know what? It's okay. God loves me anyway, faults and all. He loves me even when I have sinned and try to hide it. He loves you in the same way. He wants you to know this so you can be open and honest with Him.

It is important to be painfully honest with yourself first, so you can be completely honest with God. God sees you—all of you. Take comfort in this. Praise Him for it. Don't be like Adam and Eve. They thought they could hide what they had done from God, which broke intimacy with Him. Confess and be restored.

Like 1 Samuel 16:7 says, "The Lord looks at the heart." He sees our intentions. He sees our motives. He understands our pain. Pain is often at the heart of our choices. We do many undesirable things to try and avoid pain, which leads to guilt and shame. Yes, God knows these things, yet for our own good, we must be honest, confessing to Him the motives for our actions. This will restore intimacy with Him, relieving us of burdens. It feels good to know there is unconditional love coming our way.

A good parent, after seeing the sinful behavior of their child, cannot ignore it. There must be correction. The parent demands honesty from their child. A parent wants the child to admit to what they have done so there can be correction and restoration. This is a natural part of life. As a parent, you continue to love your child through it all. As our Heavenly Father, God will continue to love you through it all as well.

God seeing us is not a bad thing. It is a very good thing. It is such an awesome thought to know God cares for us so much and personally knows our hearts.

I praise You, Lord, for seeing me. I am known to You intimately and lovingly.

> Oh, God-of-the-Angel-Armies, no one fools you.
> You see through everyone, everything. (Jer. 20:12, MSG)

> God, investigate my life; get all the facts firsthand.
> I'm an open book to you; even from a distance, you know what I'm thinking. You know when I leave and when I get back;
> I'm never out of your sight. You know everything I'm going to say before I start the first

sentence. I look behind me and you're there, then up ahead and you're there, too—your reassuring presence, coming and going. This is too much, too wonderful—I can't take it all in!

Is there anyplace I can go to avoid your Spirit? To be out of your sight? If I climb to the sky, you're there! If I go underground, you are there! If I flew on morning's wings to the far western horizon, You'd find me in a minute—You're already there waiting! Then I said to myself, "Oh, he even sees me In the dark! At night I'm immersed in the light! It's a fact: darkness isn't dark to you; night and day, darkness and light, they're all the same to you. (Ps. 139:1–12, MSG)

S

Sabaoth—Lord of Hosts

Sacrifice—Hebrews 9:26, Hebrews 10:10

Sacred—2 Timothy 3:15

Safe—Proverbs 18:10

Salvation—Psalm 62:2, Romans 10:9–10

Same—Psalm 102:27, Hebrews 13:8

Sanctifies—Hebrews 10:10, Hebrews 2:11

Sanctuary—Psalm 73:17, Leviticus 19:30

Satisfies—Psalm 145:16, Jeremiah 31:25

Savior—Acts 5:31, 1 Timothy 4:10

Searcher—Psalm 139:23, 1 Chronicles 28:9

Security—Proverbs 3:23–26

Seeking—John 8:50

Sees—Jeremiah 20:12, 2 Chronicles 16:9

Self-Existing—Exodus 3:14

Sender—2 Chronicles 36:15–16

Serenity—Psalm 4:8

Serious—Revelation 3:19

Serving—Luke 22:27

Shalom—The Lord is Peace

Shammah—The Lord is There

Shepherd—Psalm 23, Isaiah 40:11

Shield—Psalm 59:11, Psalm 84:9

Shining—2 Corinthians 4:6

Shocking—Jeremiah 51:52–56

Shows—Romans 8:18–19

Significant—Romans 6:23

Signs—Acts 2:43, 4:30

Sincere—Romans 8:1–2

Skillful—Psalm 139:15

Slow to anger—Psalm 145:8

Smart—Genesis 18:14

Smiling—Matthew 3:16–17

Sociable—Revelation 3:20–21

Solid—Jeremiah 29:11–14

Solver—Jeremiah 31:12–14

Song—Exodus 15:2

Source—Hebrews 5:9

Sovereign—Revelation 4:8, Jeremiah 1:6

Speaks—Jeremiah 32:27

Special—1 Peter 2:24–25
Spectacular—Jeremiah 32:17–19
Spirit—Genesis 1:2, Joel
    2:28–29
Splendid/Splendor—Psalm 96:6,
    Psalm 145:4
Stable—Psalm 31:2–3
Steadfast—2 Thessalonians 3:5
Strength/Strong—Psalm 71:7
Striking—Psalm 8:1
Stronghold—Psalm 59:17, 62:6
Stunning—Revelation 5:9–14
Stupendous—Psalm 19:1
Subjects—Hebrews 2:8
Sufficient—2 Corinthians 12:9
Sumptuous—Revelation
    4:10–11
Sunrise—Luke 1:78
Superior—Jeremiah 1:19
Supplier—Philippians 4:19,
    Psalm 145:15
Supporter—Psalm 146:9
Sure—Psalm 19:7
Surpassing—Ephesians 1:19
Surprising—Genesis 8:21
Sustains—Psalm 71:6, Ruth 4:15
Sweet—Psalm 30:10–12
Swift—Isaiah 19:1, 2 Peter 2:1
Sympathetic—Psalm 55:16–19

Therapeutic

Trust God, acknowledge Him, be humble and respect Him. It will be healing and refreshing to your body. (Prov. 3:5–8; paraphrased)

I love to get a massage. It feels so good lying there for an hour listening to peaceful music, smelling essential oils while having the knots worked out. I try not to think of anything but God during this time. I send up praises asking God to do some restoration in my body and mind. Unfortunately, a massage is not something I can afford to do very often. It is a real treat when I do get to go. I always leave feeling refreshed, which is something our bodies and minds need on a regular basis.

God knows we need healing in our bodies and refreshment in our bones. He set up a way for us to get therapy without having to pay for expensive spa treatments. Here in Proverbs 3, we are told to trust God. Don't try to figure out what He is doing. Make God a part of our everyday lives. Consider Him. Talk to Him. Fellowship with Him daily, and He will keep us going down the right path. Verse 7 says not to think you have everything figured out. You don't. The danger in this is you rely on self, not God. Understand, God is King of kings and Lord of lords. Respect that. Continuing in verse 7, it says to stay away from evil of any kind. The result, verse 8, "It will be healing to your body and refreshing to your bones." It is not complicated. We just tend to make it that way.

Basically, if we allow God to be Lord over our lives, not ourselves, we can rest in the fact He knows what's best for us. That rest brings greatly desired healing and refreshment to us. If we truly trust Him, worry will dissipate. (Worry and stress do terrible things to our mind and body.) If we acknowledge God, having fellowship with Him in all we do, then He will guide us in our daily lives, giving us desired peace we need.

So you see, God is very therapeutic. He knows better than anyone how hard life is sometimes. It can take a lot out of us. He knows our bodies need a refreshing time. The Bible is full of ways God can bring this about. Psalms 23 tells of Him leading us to green pastures or a restful place. Luke 12 reminds us, God takes care of our needs.

Ponder on God's therapy. Think of the many ways God has established good things for His children. Let us praise God for being therapeutic.

I praise You, Lord, for being therapeutic. For Your curative powers. You are so caring. You know just what we need.

> Repent therefore and return, that your sins may be wiped away, in order that times of refreshing may come from the presence of the Lord. (Acts 3:19)

T

Takes—John 1:29

Tangible—John 1:14

Taste—Psalm 34:8

Teacher—Psalm 71:17, Matthew 8:19

Telling—Matthew 26:63–64, Psalm 19:1

Temple—2 Samuel 22:7, Psalm 11:4

Tender (Mercies)—Luke 1:78, Psalm 145:9

Terrific—Psalm 31:19, Job 37:22

Terrifying—Zephaniah 2:11

Territorial—Exodus 20:3–5

Therapeutic—Proverbs 3:5–8

Thorough—Hebrews 4:12–13

Timeless—Isaiah 25:8

Timely—Matthew 26:18

Tireless—Psalm 71:3, Isaiah 40:28

To be feared—Ecclesiastes 12:13

Today/Tomorrow—Revelation 4:8, Hebrews 13:8

Together—John 15:4–5

Top—Mark 5:7, Luke 2:14

Total—James 1:4–5

Touching—Luke 24:38–41

Tower of Strength—Psalm 61:3

Tranquility—Proverbs 3:1–2

Transcendence—2 Chronicles 2:6

Transforming—Philippians 3:20–21

Treasure—Matthew 6:19–21, Matthew 13:44

Tremendous—Luke 1:37

Triumphant—2 Corinthians 3:14

Triune/Trinity—John 15:26, Matthew 28:19

True—John 7:28

Truth—John 14:6, Matthew 22:16

Trustful/Trustworthy—Psalm 56:3–4, Isaiah 26:3–4

Tsidkenu—The Lord, our Righteousness

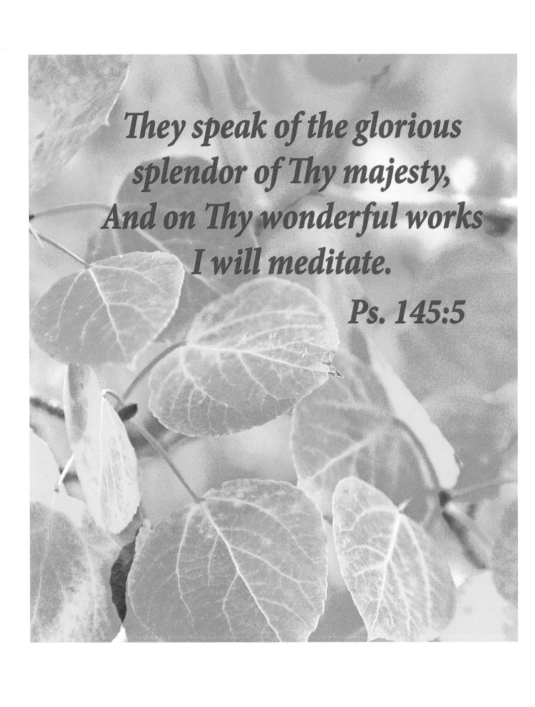

They speak of the glorious
splendor of Thy majesty,
And on Thy wonderful works
I will meditate.

Ps. 145:5

Undeniable

One generation shall praise Thy works to another, And shall declare Thy mighty acts. On the glorious splendor of Thy majesty, and on Thy wonderful works, I will meditate. And men shall speak of the power of Thine awesome acts; And I will tell of Thy greatness. (Ps. 145:4–6)

God placed within all human beings the ability to know Him personally. He also gave us the desire to worship. However, He gave us our own free will to choose to know Him personally and to choose to worship Him. He doesn't force us to praise Him, but we were created to do just that. Most people worship something or someone. It may not be God. It may be a movie star, a popular singer, or a material possession. There are many things people place their adoration on, besides God. I find it very puzzling why people choose to ignore the obvious. Proof of God's existence is everywhere, and yet they still deny Him.

Open your eyes. Take time to really notice His existence. Meditate on His splendor, His majesty, and His wonderful works. The more you notice, the more you will see, God is undeniable.

And He answered and said, "I tell you, if these become silent, the stones will cry out!" (Luke 19:40)

But He said, "If they kept quiet, the stones would do it for them, shouting praise. (Luke 19:40, MSG)

We are not meant to keep silent about praising our Heavenly Father. God placed deep within us desire to adore Him. Yes, there are many people who choose not to give God the praise and glory due His name, but if you know God at all, even if it's just a little bit, then you must praise Him. We, as God's people, are compelled too. If we don't, the Scriptures say, the stones will.

O taste and see that the Lord is good; How blessed is the man who takes refuge in Him! (Ps. 34:8)

When I was a little girl, my father worked as head gardener for our city's botanical gardens. He was amazing with plants. He could grow anything. My favorite was the peach tree he planted in our yard. The tree wasn't special to look at, but every year it grew massive peaches. My dad would have to prop the branches with sticks to keep them from breaking under the weight of the peaches.

I will never forget those beautiful, juicy, flavorful fruits. When taking a bite, the juice from the peach would run down my chin. The flavor was so sweet and delicious because they were left to ripen on the tree, then picked at the perfect time.

This is what I think of when I read Psalm 34:8, "O taste and see that the Lord is good." We can literally taste God's goodness. God was the One Who created those peaches. My dad was just a vessel to help their growth. To me, those peaches showed God's undeniable existence.

Next time you bite into something wonderful, taste and see that the Lord is good. He really is undeniable.

I praise You, God, for being undeniable.

U

Ultimate—Psalm 40:5
Unalterable—Psalm 31:3
Unchangeable—Malachi 3:6, Hebrews 6:17
Undefiled—Hebrews 7:26
Undeniable—Luke 19:40
Understanding—Jeremiah 10:12
Unequaled—Psalm 19:7–10
Unequivocal—1 John 1:5
Unerring—Deuteronomy 32:4
Unexpected—Matthew 24:36–39
Unfathomable—Romans 11:33
Uniqueness—Deuteronomy 32:39, Joel 2:27
Unsearchable—Romans 11:33, Psalm 145:3
Unstoppable—Deuteronomy 32:39–43
Untamed—Joshua 10:8–14
Upholds—Isaiah 41:10, 13
Upright—Deuteronomy 32:4, Psalm 25:8
Us—Genesis 3:22

O Lord,
God of vengence;
God of vengence,
shine forth!

Psalm 94:1

Vengeance

Have you ever praised God for vengeance? We can, and should.

> Thou who knowest, O Lord remember me, take notice of me, and take vengeance for me on my persecutors. (Jer. 15:15)

> Yet, O Lord of hosts, Thou who dost test the righteous, who seest the mind and the heart; let me see Thy vengeance on them; for to Thee I have set forth my cause. (Jer. 20:12)

Jeremiah put his trust in God to execute vengeance on his persecutors. Hebrews 10:30 reminds us that vengeance is God's. He is the one to do the repaying. I find comfort in this.

Recently I was a victim of a scam. I am not at all gullible, but this scam was very clever. The people running the scam did not get any money from me, but they did manage to access my computer and navigate around in it, until I realized what was happening. Thankfully, I only used that computer for picture editing, so they didn't get important information, but it could have been disastrous. After this happened, I was furious with these people for preying on the vulnerabilities of others. I wondered how many innocent people had fallen victim to their scam. It was very believable and seemed legitimate.

I was really mad. I had no way to expose these deceivers. The only thing I could do was to warn people about the scam. But I wanted to do more. I wanted to stop them. Then I remembered what God has said about vengeance. It is His to repay. So I began praising God for vengeance on these people. He knew who they were. I didn't. He knew how to stop them. I didn't. Now will I ever know if God chose to take vengeance on these people? Probably not. That doesn't matter. As I praised God for His vengeance, the burden was lifted from me. I felt release from my anger and desire for wrath. I rested in God and His ability to handle the situation.

God's sovereignty decides who, when, and how to carry out vengeance. It might be immediate, or it might take years. He might not carry out vengeance at all. He decides, not us. We should not take matters into our own hands.

> Never take your own revenge, beloved, but leave room for the wrath of God, for it is written, "Vengeance is mine, I will repay," says the Lord. (Rom. 12:19)

> Vengeance is Mine, and retribution, in due time their foot will slip; for the day of their calamity is near. (Deut. 32:35)

I do get angry at the injustices in this world. Sometimes I feel overwhelmed with frustration. There is so little I can do about it. Praising God for His vengeance somehow helps. It releases the burden from me and puts it on Him. It is His burden to carry. God is absolutely sovereign over all. Trust Him to know exactly what to do at exactly the right time.

I praise You, God, for Your divine vengeance.

V

Vast—Psalm 139:6–12
Vengeance—Deuteronomy 32:35, Psalm 94:1
Vigilant—Job 7:17–19
Victory—1 Chronicles 29:11
Vindicator—Deuteronomy 32:36, Psalm 54:1
Vital—John 15:4–7
Vitality (energy)—Isaiah 40:28–31
Vivid—Jeremiah 10:12–13, John 8:12
Voice—Hebrews 12:25–26

**WARRIOR:
ENGAGED IN
BATTLE**

Warrior: One engaged or experienced in battle

The Lord your God is in your midst, A victorious warrior. (Zeph. 3:17, NASB)

The Lord your God is with you. He is mighty to save. (Zeph. 3:17, NIV)

Your God is present among you. A strong warrior there to save you. (Zeph. 3:17, MSG)

God is in our midst, our victorious Warrior in battle. What battle, you may ask? It is the original battle: good vs. evil. Satan and his demons against God, His angels, and His people. A spiritual battle of epic proportions! Melodramatic? Not at all.

Ephesians 6:12 reminds us, for our struggle is not against flesh and blood but against the rulers, against the world forces of this darkness, against the spiritual forces of wickedness in the heavenly places.

As believers, we have a serious enemy, one that seeks to destroy us, or at the very least make us miserable. He is very clever at how he accomplishes this, so clever, in fact, that we forget we have a mighty Warrior on our side. We forget to praise God and call on Him in our time of trouble. Satan deceives us into believing we are on our own and that God cannot be bothered with our problems. The fact is, God has not left us alone. He is present and engaged in battle for us.

David, in the book of 1 Samuel 17, gives us a great example of trusting God as his strong Warrior. It is the story of David's defeat over Goliath. In verse 47, he said, "That all this assembly may know that the Lord does not deliver by sword or by spear; for the battle is the Lord's and He will give you into our hands." David was so confident the Lord was going to be his warrior, giving him the ability to defeat the giant, that he testified of it in front of the whole assembly.

There is another story in the book of 2 Chronicles 20, of a great multitude coming against King Jehoshaphat and Judah. The story goes, when Jehoshaphat heard of the multitude coming, he became afraid and turned his attention to the Lord. He stood in front of the assembly of Judah and praised God. In verse 6, he proclaims God in heaven and ruler over all the kingdoms of the nations: "Power and might are in Thy hand so that no one can stand against Thee." After King Jehoshaphat praises God, he petitions Him to judge the multitude. Jehoshaphat expresses their dismay but says, "Their eyes are on Thee." He acknowledged the people's trust in their God. Then in verse 15, the Lord responds to them by saying, "Do not fear or be dismayed because of this great multitude, for the battle is not yours but God's."

There are many more stories in the Bible of God being the mighty and victorious warrior. You might even have your own testimony of God as your warrior. One thing is for sure, we cannot possibly know the many battles God has fought for us in the "heavenly places." We can, however, trust He has and will keep fighting for us.

I praise You, God, for being my Warrior. I feel so blessed and reassured that the battle is Yours. I can trust You to fight for me.

The Lord is a warrior; the Lord is His name.
(Exod. 15:3)

W

Warrior—Zephaniah 3:17, Exodus 15:3
Watchful—Job 7:20
Wealth—Deuteronomy 8:18
Who Is—Revelation 4:8
Willing—Psalm 51:12
Wise/Wisdom—James 3:17
Witness—Revelation 3:14
Wonders—Acts 4:30–31
Wonderful Counselor—Isaiah 9:6
Word—John 1:1
Working—Exodus 15:11
Worthy—Revelation 4:11
Wrath—Romans 12:19, Nahum 1:2

Yahweh Nissi

And Moses built an altar, and named it, The Lord
is my Banner. (Exod. 17:15)

To praise God for being our banner, it is good to know the significance a banner can hold.

Throughout history, banners have had great military importance. First of all, they served to identify the groups of people engaging in battle. Next, large banners were used to regroup the troops after the battle. Then a banner or flag was established to claim possession of a territory. Finally, banners were used as rallying points. When a flag was flown in victory, it brought tremendous emotional responses. Psalm 20:5 says, "We will sing for joy over your victory and in the name of our God we will set up our banners." The people of the Old Testament ascribed their triumph to God by setting up banners—the banners of victory.

In Jeremiah 50:2, we see an example of how a banner was used as a rallying point. It says in verse 2, "Declare and proclaim among the nations, proclaim it and lift up a standard (banner), do not conceal it but say; Babylon has been captured."

This was a prophecy. Babylon had not been captured at this point, yet there was a command to establish a victory banner. Perhaps this was to encourage the people while intimidating the Babylonians. This would have been a bold statement, to set up a banner proclaiming victory before it even happened. A victory banner represents superiority, and the people of that time would have known the banner's significance. There would have been extreme exhilaration at the sight of unfurled banners preceding an advancing army.

Other ways banners are used is in celebrations and festivities. We raise banners to salute our favorite sports teams. We hang banners at weddings and parties announcing best wishes and love. Then there is our beloved country's flag. I have great pride in this banner. I stand and pledge my allegiance, with my hand over my heart in sincerity, to this flag.

The banner was, and still is, a large clear symbol of might and strength. When gazing at the flag, it somehow produces an emotional response of pride and joy.

If we ponder on, "The Lord is My Banner," as stated in Exodus 17:15, then it becomes clear, the people saw the Lord as the One to gaze at, knowing He is our mighty King. Our victory and triumph are in Him. When we look to the Lord, we should have a strong emotional response of love, trust, and security.

I like to picture myself waving the Lord's banner of love over me, like I'd wave a banner of my favorite team at a football game. I'm even more proud to wave this banner.

In the Song of Solomon 2:4, the Shulammite women was talking about Solomon when she said, "And his banner over me is love." In other words, everyone could clearly see, Solomon loved her. It was not hidden.

If the Lord is your banner, then remember, His love over you is not hidden. If you like to think in military terms, then know, He is your victorious King. If you prefer to think of the banner as celebratory, then enjoy the Lord and celebrate all He has done for you.

I praise You, Yahweh Nissi. The Lord is my banner!

X, Y, Z

Yahweh—Exodus 3:14
Yahweh Nissi—The Lord, my Banner—Exodus 17:15
Yahweh Yireh—The Lord will provide—Genesis 22:14
Yes—2 Corinthians 1:19–20

Zeal—Isaiah 9:7, Zephaniah 3:8

About the Author

Kimberlee Hutcherson is a photographer living in Pagosa Springs, Colorado. She has resided there along with her husband, Chris, for forty years. Born in Madison, Wisconsin. Left there at age twelve. She has four children and, currently, four grandchildren. What brings her joy, apart from her walk with the Lord, is her wonderful family, photography, skiing, and fishing.